The Interactive Field in Analysis

Murray Stein, editor

Volume One

CW00553144

Chiron Publications • Wilmette, Illinois

The Chiron Clinical Series
ISBN 0-933029-77-2

General Editor: Murray Stein
Book Review Editor: Boris Matthews

© 1995 by Chiron Publications. All rights reserved. No part of this publication may be reproduced, stored in a retrieval system, or transmitted in any form, by any means, electronic, mechanical, photocopying, recording, or otherwise, without the prior written permission of the publisher, Chiron Publications, 400 Linden Avenue, Wilmette, Illinois 60091.

Printed in the United States of America.

Book design by Elaine Hill.

Library of Congress Cataloging-in-Publication Data

The interactive field in analysis / Murray Stein, editor.
    p. cm. — (The Chiron clinical series)
    Includes bibliographical references
    ISBN 0-933029-77-2 :
    1. Psychoanalysis. 2. Jung, C. G. (Carl Gustav), 1875-1961.
    3. Psychoanalytic counseling. 4. Psychoanalytic interpretation.
    I. Stein, Murray, 1943-   . II. Series.
    BF17.I56   1995
    150.19'54—dc20   94-41370
                                                                          CIP

Other books from The Chiron Clinical Series

Mad Parts of Sane People in Analysis
Murray Stein, editor

Transference/Countertransference
Nathan Schwartz-Salant and Murray Stein, editors

Contents

On the Interactive Field as the Analytic Object

Nathan Schwartz-Salant

Introduction

Today, the notion of a "third area" or "field" between analyst and analysand is rapidly gaining importance in many schools of psychoanalysis. This idea—whether expressed in terms of Winnicott's "transitional" or "potential space" (1971), Greene's concept of the "analytic object" (1975), various approaches of self psychologists, notably Stolorow and his colleagues, to an "intrasubjective field" (1987), or Ogden's "analytic third" (1994), to mention several major contributions—is based on the combined subjectivities of analyst and analysand.[1] By contrast, C. G. Jung's fundamental way of dealing with the analytic process rested upon his notion of the collective unconscious. M.-L. von Franz has further extended Jung's ideas by determining that the collective unconscious has a fieldlike quality, "the excited points of which are the archetypes" (1980, p. 61). In *Number and Time*, she states that the field is the latent source of

Nathan Schwartz-Salant, Ph.D., is a Jungian analyst, trained in Zurich, and in private practice in New York City and Princeton, New Jersey. He is the author of *Narcissism and Character Transformation, The Borderline Personality: Vision and Healing*, and numerous clinical papers. He is president of the Salant Foundation and director of the Center for Analytical Perspectives.

the form all our perceptions, behaviors, and thinking (1974, p. 154). In this approach, it is the objective nature of the collective unconscious that is dominant. Jung sees an individual's subjectivity engaging this archetypal level to reveal the meaning or quality of a given moment. This means that one can experience aspects of the dynamic properties of a field that is transcendent to one's individual consciousness.

There is yet another way of viewing the role of a field in analytic practice. The psychoanalytic approach deals with the subjectivities between two people, and analytical psychology deals with the intersection of an individual's subjectivity and the archetypal processes of the collective unconscious, but it is possible to do both—not to exclude one while engaging the other. In fact, it is by combining both that two people can become aware of how their individual processes participate in and are affected by the objectivity of the collective unconscious. In this conception of a field, personal, historical acquisitions—object relations—mix and combine with an objective substratum, Jung's collective unconscious. One becomes aware that the field has its own dynamics, which are separate from and independent of the individuals. Yet the discovery of these dynamics is only possible by experiencing them through the individual and combined subjectivities of both people. The experience of this awareness is in and of itself deeply healing. Such a notion of the field—an understanding of which actively includes both subjective and objective dimensions—can be called the *interactive field*.[2] The interactive field is *in between* the field of the collective unconscious and the realm of subjectivity, while at the same time including them both.

All forms of analysis will generally differentiate opposites in the analytic process. Whether it be through noting the difference between the analysand's conscious and unconscious attitudes, or between projected contents and defenses, or as opposing attributes of internal structure, or of transference dynamics, opposites play a central role in all analytic thinking. Thinking and working in terms of opposites is an essential attribute of Jung's approach to the psyche. But it is the manner in which the opposites are dealt with that will distinguish an approach recognizing the field to have its own objective process from an approach that considers the field to be composed only of the combined subjectivities of analyst and analysand from which one can extract information about the analysand's personal history. That is, one approach assumes that the only viable analytical concern is with subjectivity, i.e., previous history, while the other includes this but considers it to be a wave on a greater sea of objective process (Jung 1946, par. 354). This latter approach opens the possibility of experiencing the field's processes, which are not necessarily traceable to the analysand's personal history. Such processes may also be archetypal, transpersonal dominants that usually interface with historical contents derived from object relations.

Space prohibits discussing the field approaches based upon subjectivity in detail, so I shall confine myself to Ogden's position concerning a "third area" between analyst and analysand. Discussing the "analytic third" in his book *Subjects of Analysis*, Ogden writes:

> The analytic process reflects the interplay of three subjectivities: the subjectivity of the analyst, of the analysand, and of the analytic third. The analytic third is the creation of the analyst and analysand, and at the same time the analyst and analysand (qua analyst and analysand) are created by the analytic third. (There is no analyst, no analysand, no analysis in the absence of the third.)
>
> Because the analytic third is experienced by analyst and analysand in the context of his or her own personality system, personal history, psychosomatic makeup, and so on, the experience of the third (although jointly created) is not identical for each participant. Moreover, the analytic third is an asymmetrical construction because it is generated in the context of the analytic setting, which is powerfully defined by the relationship roles of analyst and analysand. As a result, the unconscious experience of the analysand is privileged in a specific way, that is, it is the past and present experience of the analysand that is taken by the analytic pair as the principal (although not exclusive) subject of the analytic discourse. The analyst's experience in and of the analytic third is (primarily) utilized as a vehicle for the understanding of the conscious and unconscious experience of the analysand. (1994, pp. 93–94)

This understanding of the analytic third gives more scope to the analyst's reflections than is afforded by the idea that the analyst introjects the analysand's process and then, through reverie and reflection upon the induced countertransference, gives the analysand's process a new form, for example, through an interpretation. In Ogden's approach, the third always functions in the process, affecting both analyst and analysand in a way that is not exhausted by understanding and thus allows for a greater creativity and search for truth than do the previous models of analysis.

But due to the collective unconscious, a universal substratum of existence, there is a degree of objectivity for the processes in the third area, and this results in its fieldlike quality. Much of alchemical science, which Jung explored for nearly fifty years, was devoted to proceeding in ways that increased the probability of gaining access to the deeper dynamics of the field. According to Jung and von Franz, the key to understanding this lies in a qualitative view of *number*. "Natural numbers appear to represent the typical, universally recurring, common motion patterns of both psychic *and* physical energy" (von Franz 1974, p. 166).

The numerical proposition that especially pertains to field dynamics is called the "Axiom of Maria." Jung has dealt with it in numerous places (1944, 1946, 1955), as has von Franz (1974, 1980), and I have also discussed it with special reference to the clinical issue of projective identification (1989). The axiom, an example of the qualitative logic of prescientific cultures, is as follows: "Out of the One comes the Two, out of the Two comes the Three, and from the Three comes the Fourth as the One." "One" signifies a state prior to an established order, for example, the Chaos of alchemy; it can also represent the way an analytic session is experienced in its opening phase.

Most forms of analysis accomplish the first stage in which "Out of the One comes the Two." Typically, the analyst may become aware of thoughts or feelings, body states, or perhaps a tendency to wander mentally and lose focus. Such states of mind can reflect the same states in the analysand. The analyst, depending on the extent of his or her own self-knowledge, could become aware of their induced quality and employ this for understanding the analysand's process. This is the well-known process of the concordant (Racker) or syntonic (Fordham) countertransference. Another possibility is that the analyst's states of mind or body represent an opposite or complementary state to the analysand's, what Racker calls the complementary countertransference. In both instances, the analyst follows a movement of One becoming Two. In the first case, the analyst has achieved an awareness of syntonic opposites: the same quality exists in the analyst's and the analysand's psyche. In the second case, the analyst's psyche contains one quality and the analysand's contains the opposite. For example, the analyst may experience a tendency to talk without much restraint, and the analysand may feel gripped by a silence; or the analyst may feel depressed, while a manic quality dominates the analysand; the analyst may feel disgust or hatred, and the analysand may be filled with feelings of love and attraction. Generally, any pair of opposites may register in this way.

Let us imagine an example of engaging the field's dynamics

with a syntonic-like countertransference reaction. Suppose that while I am with a client I feel anxiety. Whose anxiety is it? I can wonder if it is an introject, part of a process of projective identification. Or is the anxiety my own? Does the anxiety stem from my psyche or from the analysand? The simple positing of this set of questions leads me to wonder if I am dealing with a set of opposites. This would be a pair of opposites of the same quality, that is, anxiety. They would be experienced as consecutive aspects of a process in which the anxiety is alternately felt as my own subjective state and then as the analysand's condition.[3]

Normally, in the analytic tradition, an analyst having gone through such a process of reflection will come to a conclusion as to whose anxiety is essentially at issue, as in the processing of projective identification. But we have the option here of suspending judgment and experiencing both possibilities simultaneously. As Jung describes, "the opposites become a vessel in which what was previously now one thing and now another floats vibratingly, so that the painful suspension between opposites gradually changes into the bilateral activity of the point in the centre" (1955, par. 296). To do this, one must be willing to sacrifice the power of knowing "whose content" one is dealing with and instead imagine that the content, here anxiety, exists in the field itself and does not necessarily belong to either person. The content can be imaginally thrust into the field that analyst and analysand occupy together so that it becomes a "third thing." [4] Thus, in keeping with the Axiom of Maria, "out of the Two comes the Three" not as an interpretation but as a field quality. At such moments, analyst and analysand are both in the analytic crucible. I believe it is this sacrifice of "knowing" that can enliven the field and bring forth its deeper, archetypal dimension (Schwartz-Salant, 1991). As in Jung's idea of active imagination, one can continue to focus on the field itself, as though it were an object. The field becomes a *presence* that both people are inside of and, simultaneously, observers of.

At this point in our imaginary example, when I focus upon this anxiety, now felt as a bilateral point, a "third," and as I allow it to intensify through my own concentration, something changes. It is as if I am now inside the anxiety and, alternatively, it is in me; an oscillation occurs that the analysand can feel as well. The sense of space or atmosphere has changed. Everything that is now said is felt through the lens of anxiety that belongs to neither of us but is a *presence* that we are both inside of, and viewers of, as if it were also an object. In fact, any emotion can oscillate between being experienced as an object one studies and reflects upon, and being experienced from within, by direct encounter with the emotion itself. In this latter state, the emotion becomes a container pervaded by a sense of "Oneness." The alchemical idea that there are two forms to any given substance (such as sulphur, lead, or water), one being "ordinary" and the other "philosophical," stems perhaps from ways that affects can be experienced both as "things" and as containing states of wholeness.[5]

While "whose anxiety" is sorted out in this way, it is never the end result but rather the Three on the way to the Fourth in which a mystery of containment is known. Within this crucible it becomes possible for an analysand to experience, for example, anxiety concerning engulfment and identity loss with me and to recognize how this repeats such fusion fears with the analysand's mother. The container makes it possible for the analyst and analysand to become both objective observers and participants of the affect that is present and enlivened. This gives the opportunity to experience the effects and dynamics of the affective states and especially provides the possibility to test the ways in which one tends to experience the affect in one's life and the behavior patterns it elicits, and to explore a host of associative material which thus may be stimulated. It is the "vessel" and the paradox of process that we thus seek, for this, and this alone, can contain the mysterious, mad aspects of our being, indeed regain their mystery, and allow for a felt experience of the relation between the world known through "parts" and their link to a larger sphere of oneness (see Jung 1955, par. 662).

This example, as far as I have given it, does not depart in its essentials from the psychoanalytic ideas of subjectivity as a third area. Winnicott's idea of transitional space has the same topological quality as the *vas hermeticum*. It is what occurs for the participants afterward that distinguishes the notion of the interactive field. For example, a state of joining can be experienced by both parties—not a fusing that blurs boundaries, but a rhythmic process in which the field itself is felt to have its own dynamic that pulls both people toward each other but also separates them. It is as if any tendencies toward literalization are annulled by the field itself.

This experience is akin to what the ancients called the sacred marriage, and what in alchemy is known as the *coniunctio*. Experiencing it opens one to the sense of mystery that can be transformative, much as a vision or "big" dream can be fateful. In this there is a mutuality of shared process, and we depart somewhat from Ogden's caution that "analyst and analysand are not engaged in a democratic process of mutual analysis" (1994, pp. 93–94). While the asymmetry of the analytic process must never be forgotten, there are also important times of shared experience, when experiencing the transference is more essential than interpreting it. This gives the analysand more courage to experience fusion desires and fears; the analysand can begin to see that there is a union process beyond death through fusion. This process has an archetypal dimension, and the experience of its *numinosum* has a great deal to do with healing.

Consider a case in which I frequently experienced a tendency to talk while the analysand appeared frozen in silence—an example of the complementary countertransference. In alchemical terms, this can be understood as that aspect of the process in which the One becomes the Two. We experienced completely opposite states, one the desire or need to be completely closed off and silent, the other talking and almost compulsively trying to connect and be creative. To begin with, for either of us it became a task to recognize that there was a pair of opposites at work. Once acknowledged, I could use this dyadic level of opposites to make an interpretation. For example, the third could be an awareness that my patient was reexperiencing, in the transference, the actual historical trauma of her father's manic desires to rob her of her creativity and the very fabric of her sense of self. This kind of awareness was of great value, for it brought to the surface a terrible interactive process that the analysand had been repressing but which had been affecting her whole life in significant ways. She either avoided creativity or became gripped by a mania whenever she attempted to allow her creativity expression.

I could, however, choose to forgo such knowledge and to sacrifice it to the state of "unknowing," allowing the unknown to become the focus. I could then ask a silent question: What is the nature of the field between us, what is our unconscious dyad like? In this manner, we opened to the field as to an object. In the process, the opposites—manic speech and silence—shifted. I was now in the grip of silence and the analysand had one new thought after another. The awareness of opposites oscillated until a new center was felt, Jung's "bilateral point," and from this focus the field itself began to come alive. The opposites could be further seen to have been only separable fragments of a far deeper fantasy. We discovered primal scene fantasies in which manic speech was a sublimated form of a dangerous phallus, and the opposite, the silence, was a putrefied corpse, the remains of her body killed by envy. While such images may be historical, for example, in the sense of what the analysand unconsciously experienced through her father's fantasy and her reaction or pertaining to actual physical or sexual abuse, the field itself has archetypal processes that are different from such historical levels, as important as they may be.

Seeing and experiencing the affects and imagery of each person—in his or her own way—of an unconscious dyad, in its archaic and destructive form, can result in its changing into a more positive couple. On the one hand, this could be seen as a dyad that had also been present in the analysand's history. But here something else is possible. The move from Two to Three can, instead of resulting in a historically based interpretation, become a new experience of the field. As in the previous example, *analyst and analysand can become subject to the field.* That is to say, giving up the power or knowledge *about* another person can leave one in the position of focusing on and being affected by the field itself. This can involve experiencing less archaic forms, which can lead to liberating insights. One's subjectivity enhances the field, and its objectivity interacts with the analyst and the analysand. A different kind of Three (as previously noted) can then emerge in which the opposites are transcended. This can be a union state, the alchemical *coniunctio.* At this stage, one can often feel a current inherent in the field in which one feels alternately pulled toward, then separated from the other person. This is the rhythm of the *coniunctio* as a Three quality of the field becoming Four. "The number four constitutes a 'field' with an internal closed rhythmical movement that proceeds to fan out from the center (and) contracts back to the center" (von Franz 1974, p. 124). Furthermore, the move from Three to Four is one in which a sense of finiteness is felt. The level of "Threeness" does not have the felt boundaries of the Four. In a sense, the level of Three calls out for interpretation as an expansive act, but perhaps also as one that defends the analyst against the kind of intimacy that can evolve in the movement to "Fourness." In the movement to "Four" the observer's *wholeness* becomes involved, leading to the paradoxical sense of a subjective objectivity (ibid., p. 122).

The analysand's psyche still contains the previous image of an actual or imaginal violation. How does this change? Surely not from overlaying a new image or from recalling remnants of some positive fantasy life that also existed. The negative, destructive fusion state is too powerful to be affected by historical recall of other states. Can one imagine a process that actually extracts, dissolves, or transforms the prior image, be it, for example, an engram of an actual, abusive history or an introjected primal scene trauma?

It is here that field dynamics play a role in ways that especially differ from field ideas based on subjectivity alone. Experiencing the field and being changed by its process is a way of transforming internal structures. New forms that order affects, which were previously overwhelming and fragmenting, can come into existence. Field dynamics also play a central role in the process of incarnating archetypal experience into an internal, felt reality. One may take the view that every child knows levels of the *numinosum* at birth and then loses this awareness to one degree or another, depending on how the mother-child dyad is able to contain its sacred presence. The mother is the first carrier, in projection, of this spiritual energy for the child, but the child may have known it before the projection process occurs. Or one may take the view that there are spiritual levels that have never been conscious to an individual in any manner yet can break in from the collective unconscious. In either approach, one is often left with the dilemma of an awareness of the *numinosum* that is then lost to the demands of life in space and time and to the inertia of matter. This awareness still lives in the unconscious, either as a level of "paradise lost" or as a spiritual potential that the soul innately knows exists, and the age-old problem of its incarnation into a felt center of psyche remains. Experiencing the interactive field has the capacity to facilitate this incarnating process.

In addition, it is also possible, at moments, to perceive an imaginal reality that seems to be a property of the field itself. This is like experiencing the time-quality of the moment. One may become conscious of an image that is felt to emerge out of the field and reflect the states of both people. Each person may offer his or her sense of the imagery of the field as he or she focuses upon it, similar to Jung's conception of active imagination. The result may resemble a "dialogue drawing" in which a sense of the field is constructed from the imagery each person creates. Interpretation in the classical sense of relating imagery and affect to early developmental issues blocks this awareness of the field. Interpretation here takes another form: intensely experiencing the quality of the moment in the field, sometimes verbalizing the experience and sometimes remaining silent. The active, conscious experiencing of the energies and patterns that can be perceived in the field, experiencing them in the here-and-now, appears to affect the field, enlivening it as if it were a living organism. The field can suffer: tears and sadness can feel nearly literally present. At other moments, it is nearly impossible to attend to the field. Extremely chaotic states of mind (in either person) can make it very difficult to allow the field to be the object, let alone perceive any imagery.

If we engage the field, we can become aware of a deep organizing process of which we were previously unconscious. One may sense or intuit this as a process that is ongoing but not necessarily known in the space-time realm the ego usually occupies. The field has the paradoxical nature of being created through the act of submission to it, while also being an ever-present *increatum*, a process out of time. To enter the imaginal world of the field requires that one give up ego control to a high degree. To enter it is neither to fuse with another person nor to split one's ego into an irrational experiencing-fusing part and a rational observing part. Something more is needed, a desire to experience the field in ways that may surely reveal the limitation of any conception one had of the state of meaning of a particular analytic interaction. Through faith in a larger process, one often discovers that the particular form of the field is actually far more archaic and powerful than anything one had imagined. This experience of the existing form, and the creation/discovery of new forms, can have a transformative effect on internal structure and can allow new structures to incarnate.

Dangers Associated with Employing the
Interactive Field Concept in Analytic Practice

There are dangers inherent in this approach to the interactive field. The alchemists often said that their "elixir" or "stone" was both a poison and a cure; the field as a "third thing" with its own objectivity can also be just that.

The interactive field creates a wide spectrum of states that extends from experiences of an intense erotic current and desire for literalization to states of emotional and mental deadness and a total lack of connection. Since these latter states are so problematic for the pain they create and the wounding they inflict—especially upon the analyst's narcissism—their opposite, in which erotic currents can appear to create intense fields of union and a deep knowing of the other, become extremely seductive. The analyst can focus upon them, for example, by recalling past experiences and/or unconsciously imagining them. Such acts have a strong, induced affect, and they may be used to avoid feeling the dark states of mind that generally follow the *coniunctio*.

The *coniunctio* that can form from the unconscious psyches of both people can be of a positive or negative nature. Jung recognized that the experience of the *coniunctio* can lead to the creation of kinship libido (1946, par. 445) and thus beyond the transference illusion. The problem is that there are many forms of the *coniunctio*, and while a field of desire may accompany a number of them, the erotics of the field cannot be properly assessed without an awareness of the structural quality of the unconscious couple. For example, the fifth woodcut of the *Rosarium* comprises two figures, each participating in the act of coitus. But in another, earlier alchemical text, the *Turba Philosophorum*, the couple has a different form (Jung 1955, par. 15). Here the two figures are intertwined in a violent fusion state leading to death, and the passion accompanying this image does not have the modulation and control of the passion represented in the *Rosarium*. In both cases, the erotic quality must be seen as a field quality and not something to own or identify with. In clinical practice, one often finds that more conscious, loving connections, while genuine, are also ways of covering a far more dangerous fusion field, often linked to issues of early abuse. Just as sexuality can hide anxiety in the transference, sexuality can hide a monstrous dimension of the unconscious couple.

I have been consulted by analysts in several cases years after their completion wherein the analysts reported that although the treatment ended in a seemingly good manner, they were intermittently contacted by their ex-analysands, who reported feeling tormented for years afterward. These analysands were not suffering the pain of having concretized, actually lived out, the erotic energies of the *coniunctio*, for there was no actual sexual acting-out. Rather it was crucial to them that the analysts involved recognized and expressed that *they too* suffered the sacrifice involved in maintaining boundaries. The analysts had done a good job as far as boundaries were concerned, but their countertransference resistance to also feeling the pain of losing the erotic connection they too had felt left the analysand in a terrible quandary. The analysts had split off these feelings, and in reality the analysand was left holding all of the pain, rage, and despair of a union that could not be consummated. These analysands were freed from this torment only when, several years later, they briefly resumed analysis, and the analysts could own and register their own suffering over the same issue.

But the greatest dangers of working within a shared field arise if the analyst believes that the *coniunctio* is the goal of the work. Even a developed form of the *coniunctio*—the kind in the *Rosarium* where literalization is self-contained by the field dynamics themselves—must not be the main emphasis. Rather, one's focus must also be on the *nigredo*, the dark, disordering state that follows all *coniunctio* states. Alchemical literature is a mine of information on this point. All transformation, insist the alchemists, happens through the death and putrefaction which follow a union state. If an analyst knows this, and is willing to seek out affects of withdrawal, absence, confusion, deadness, and emptiness, after a session that has achieved a union state, an I-Thou connection, he or she will usually be on a safe path. One cannot emphasize enough that the *nigredo*, the death of structure and the terrifying affects usually associated with the mad parts that surface, is the prized substance of analysis, as it was for the alchemists. A strong negative transference or negative countertransference accompanies the *nigredo*, and it is precisely here that the analyst can misuse the previous experiences of union as a way to avoid experiencing intense negative affects and the associated painful states of mind. The analyst may either attempt to recreate the union or act out anger at its absence by passively identifying with the dissociative nature of the field quality of the *nigredo*. Instead, its affects must be sought out amid their mildest currents, which is not an easy task when the far more pleasant, blissful state of union has just preceded them. I believe it is this respect for the *dynamics of the field*, in which union states and the death of structure are encountered in succession, that is our best guide to employing the field concept safely and to respecting its archetypal dimension. Countertransference resistance is the problem, in analysis in general, but it is especially heightened in a mutual field experience. If the analyst will seek out his or her negative feelings after an experience of union with the analysand, or if the analyst will register such negative feelings and reflect that some level of *coniunctio* may have unconsciously occurred, then the *nigredo* may become the focus of the work.

While an analyst's resistance to the *nigredo* renders the field approach dangerous in the extreme, another danger must also be noted, namely that a person suffering from a dissociative disorder is always, to one degree or another, in a trance state. The field approach itself tends to constellate a mild hypnotic state. As a result, serious errors can be committed, not by what one does through action alone—that is easy enough to proscribe—but through what one says and even what one imagines, for the analyst's unconscious tends to be acutely experienced by the dissociated analysand, as if by an enhanced capacity for ESP. Generally, the dissociated analysand tends to hear the analyst's statements in a very literal way while the analyst believes he or she is speaking in metaphors. This is particularly dangerous when the analyst is sidestepping negative affects and can use the binding power of processes in the third area, the interactive field, to split these affects off by forcing the existence of rapport where, in fact, the main quality of the interaction is a lack of connection. Only if the analyst is alert to the process of dissociation can he or she even begin to consider dealing with processes as an interactive field. Often years of work with an analysand must first transpire in which dissociative states are dealt with, and only then can the field be experienced with any measure of safety.

The Transformation of Structure or Form: Reflections on an Alchemical Text

The interactive field is a conception that hearkens back to ancient alchemical ideas. In these early centuries, culminating in Renaissance alchemy, the problem of *form* or structure was paramount: how is the form of an object created and how does it change? How does a seed become a tree, and how does a metal with a given structure change to another metal, as in the ancient alchemical dream of lead becoming gold? Because all schools of thought in analytic practice attempt to create new forms of internal structure, this emphasis upon a change in form especially links psychotherapy to its roots in the work of fifteenth- and sixteenth-century alchemists who prefigured the discovery of the psyche (Jung 1955, par. 150). In Kleinian thought, one deals with a movement from the so-called Paranoid schizoid position (Ps) to the Depressive position (Dp). For example, a person dominated by the splitting processes and affects of Ps will often react with a rage that distorts reality in a given situation, while someone who has been able to enter Dp will experience the same situation with much more tolerance and a capacity to see the reality of another person's complaint. A self psychologist will be interested in, among other changes, the transformation of a sadistic superego into a benevolent, idealized form and the development of self-objects from primitive to more adapted forms. A Freudian will be interested in changes in ego development represented by a movement from an oral to an anal and phallic-genital stage, all of which represent different forms of psychic organization. A Jungian will focus on individuation and its myriad changing internal forms; and an object relations clinician considers, for instance, the creation of psychic structures acquired by passage through stages of separation and rapprochement. These schools of thought all reflect models that are representations of change in the structural form of the psyche.

The main result of experiencing the field's processes is the transformation of internal structure. To see further how the alchemists thought about this process, consider the *Splendor Solis* (1582) (McLean 1981). Second in significance only to the *Rosarium Philosophorum* (1550) (McLean 1980), which was the centerpiece of Jung's study of the transference, the *Splendor Solis* deals with issues that complement the *Rosarium*, notably the problem of the embodiment of archetypal processes. In the beginning of the text, we find a preface composed of several treatises. The First Treatise describes the "Origin of the Stone of the Ancients and how it is Perfected through Art." We are told that the form of the thing to be created, the "Stone of the Wise," can only come from Nature. "Nature serves Art, and then again Art serves Nature. . . . It knows what kind of formation is agreeable to Nature, and how much of it should be done by Art, so that through Art this Stone may attain its form. Still, the form is from Nature: for the actual form of each and every thing that grows, animate or metallic, arises out of the inner power of the material" (McLean 1981, p. 10). By "Nature" we can understand the psyche, and by "Art" the conscious attitudes and techniques of analysis.

We then find an especially interesting and unusually clear example of alchemical science:

> It should however be noted that the essential form cannot arise in the material. It comes to pass through the operation of an accidental form: not through the latter's power, but by the power of another active substance such as fire, or some other warmth acting upon it. Hence we use the allegory of a hen's egg, wherein the essential form of the putrefaction arises without the accidental form, which is a mixture of the red and the white, by the power of warmth which works on the egg from the brood hen.

And although the egg is the material of the hen, nevertheless no form arises therein, either essential or accidental, except through putrefaction. (McLean 1981, p. 12)

We can extract several key ideas. First, an "accidental form" is necessary, and this form is a "mixture of the red and the white." This alludes to the *coniunctio* of king and queen, sol and luna, or in analysis, to the unconscious marriage of aspects of each person's unconscious, where one psyche contributes the active "red substance" and the other a more receptive "white substance"; these roles also can change. The form is said to be "accidental," which means it is acausal; its existence is not caused by any previous operation. The passage further says that the form emerging in the material being worked with does so without the power of the "accidental form," and with the power of an active substance, such as fire. This implies that the "accidental form" that arises from the union of opposites does not necessarily mediate its properties through a phenomenon of energy. We have a similar idea in the theory of Rupert Sheldrake concerning the creation and stability of form, wherein "morphic fields" are not transmitted by energy but instead carry information (1991, p. 111). But how is the "accidental form" still essential? The text answers that it is a precondition for the creative death of structure, the putrefaction that is the secret of transformation. An active process, expending energy is also involved, as in the allegory of the brood hen's heat. I have noted that this is akin to the energy one puts into dealing with the generally intense negative transference and countertransference reactions, such as tendencies toward withdrawal and mental blankness that often follow the *coniunctio*, but which may also be readily sidestepped.

The question arises: Since the "accidental form"—the *coniunctio*—has no direct bearing in the process in the way of some affect of transmission of power in some manner, why not forget about its existence and only attend to what has an actual effect? I think psychotherapy has, in essence, followed this path. The "accidental" union state is treated as a hidden parameter. Jung notes that the *coniunctio* is usually only known to have occurred in a session from dreams that follow it (1946, par. 461). Alchemical science attempted to imaginally engage the process that would encourage the creation of such an accidental form, which in turn may have the resonance effects Sheldrake postulates (1991, pp. 110f.). But the union state itself will generally not forge a new internal structure unless one faces and integrates some of the chaos to which it leads.

Through the *nigredo,* the alchemists attempted to purify themselves from the ever-present regressive desires to identify with archetypal processes, such as the *coniunctio*. This purification, achieved through numerous *coniunctio-nigredo* sequences, and thus through much suffering, was symbolically imaged by the death of the dragon, itself representing the drive toward concretization. It must be understood that such drives, for example, toward the concretization of instinctual processes, are not located only in the subjectivities of either person. They are also aspects of the field itself, especially as it attempts to become incarnate in space and time. Thus it is not only individuals who are changed: the field they occupy also takes on new forms.

With an understanding of the properties that the background field manifests, we can engage its dynamics and be changed in the process. This is the essence of this approach: Interpretation and the changes interpretation sets in motion is not the transformative feature, nor is empathy and its vicissitudes of imperfection. Rather, change (and this essentially means a change in the internal, structural form of a psyche) is created by experiencing over and over again the quality of a moment in time and its meaning, much as one is affected by a vision.

The Effect of Differing Attitudes to the *Nigredo*

While two people can experience the *coniunctio,* how they process it will vary as a function of their subjectivity. For example, two people may experience a union state and know of its existence directly as a "here and now" state. Or they may not consciously register its existence, but the following night the analysand may dream of a wedding. Furthermore, in the next session, the relationship between analyst and analysand may have shifted from one that was filled with a sense of connection to one that is dominated by an absence of relationship and even states of schizoid withdrawal and mental deadness. One analyst may see this as a need to withdraw from the closeness of the previous session because of the analysand's attachment disorder and resultant reaction to the prior connection; another analyst may see the reaction to a felt connection to be a significant measure of an underlying schizoid or borderline quality in the analysand. But an analyst who is focused upon a *field dynamic*—the point of view that a field has been created between them through their subjectivities intersecting with the field quality of the collective unconscious, a field which has its own dynamics—may also see the state of deadness and withdrawal as a natural concomitant of the previous union state. He or she may recognize, from this point of view, that these dark qualities are not only a representative of developmental failures but would exist for any individual psyche that has felt the union state. Furthermore, the analyst would see this union state and the resulting *nigredo* as the essential rhythm of transformation. In turn, he or she would provide a different relationship to these states, and to their containment, than would be provided by any interpretation in developmental terms. Rather than seeing the analysand's problems with the depressive position, or rapprochement issues, or fears of engulfment or the like, the analyst would note and experience the field dynamics involved. This can have the same kind of containing quality that exists in many cases of extreme anxiety when the analyst knows, from experience, that these states are part of a larger, potentially positive process. Then the *nigredo* can begin to work toward its purpose of dissolving old structures, especially introjects that do not accord well with the analysand's essence. In a sense, this is a process in which new forms are created in the analysand, and perhaps analyst as well, and within the space they occupy. Forms that can contain and process what had been severely disordering affects can come into existence through experiencing the field and its dynamics.

Thus, how we think about fields matters a great deal. As a mere metaphor for a combined subjectivity, they are useful but essentially there to reflect the analysand's history as it unfolds in the analytic process. But considered as being archetypally created along with the combined subjectivity of both people and having dynamics that extend beyond the subjective nature of the parts combined, the idea of an interactive field can lead to different ways of conceiving the analytic process. In general, the field when seen only as comprising of the combined subjectivities of analyst and analysand is a special case of the larger, objectively toned, interactive field concept.

The Field as the Analytic Object

In his paper "Recommendations to Physicians Practising Psycho-analysis," Freud gives advice which is as pertinent today as it was in 1912, although now his optimism seems almost quaint.

> The first problem confronting an analyst who is treating more than one patient a day will seem to him the hardest. It is the task of keeping in mind all the innumerable names, dates, detailed memories and pathological products which each patient communicates in the course of months and years of treatment, and not confusing them with similar material produced by other patients. . . . If one is required to analyze six, eight, or even more patients daily, the feat of memory involved in achieving this will provoke incredulity, astonishment. . . . Curiosity will in any case be felt about the technique which makes it possible to master such an abundance of material. . . .
>
> The technique, however, is a very simple one. . . . It rejects the use of any special expedient (even that of taking notes). It consists simply in not directing one's notice to anything in particular and in maintaining the same "evenly-suspended attention" . . . in the face of all that one hears. In this way we spare ourselves a strain on our attention which could not in any case be kept up for several hours daily, and we avoid a danger which is inseparable from the exercise of deliberate attention. For as soon as anyone deliberately concentrates his attention to a certain degree, he begins to select from the material before him. . . . This, however, is precisely what must not be done. . . .
>
> What is achieved in this manner will be sufficient for all requirements during the treatment. Those elements of the material which already form a connected context will be at the doctor's conscious disposal; the rest, as yet unconnected and in chaotic disorder, seems at first to be submerged, but rises readily into recollection as soon as the patient brings something new to which it can be related. (1912, p. 111f)

Freud's advice has been long recognized as often difficult to follow. Many clinicians have recognized the reason: as long as areas of meaninglessness, emptiness, mindlessness or blankness, overwhelming and fragmenting anxiety, intense despair and often envy are constellated, it is nearly impossible to maintain an evenly suspended attention. Or, to put it differently, when the analysand's psychotic parts are activated, the analyst's capacity to maintain an even, free-floating attention is challenged to the utmost. He or she might as well attempt to enter a deep, tranquil state of meditation in the New York City subway at rush hour.

When Bion began to investigate psychotic states of mind, he discovered just how difficult it was to attain the state Freud recommends. Bion recognized that an essential element of faith was needed during this attempt. This notion of an act-of-faith became one of his central ideas. Donald Meltzer comments:

> The idea of free-floating attention seems to be a simple one, conceived as simple to accomplish, on the model of free-floating in water. . . . The child may be required to exercise an act of faith in letting go of daddy or trying to swim . . . but that is based on experience of daddy's good will already in

hand. Bion's act-of-faith would correspond more to floating free in shark-infested waters. It assumes that everyone has a fiend following him, is on the verge of hallucinosis, megalomania, delusions, catastrophic anxiety. . . . The question must arise, is it really possible to do such a thing. . . . Bion seems to suggest that this belief is contingent on the realization of the fiend in one's own mind, that hallucinosis, megalomania, delusion exist and are merely held at bay by some means. . . . The sharks that infest (Bion's) waters are lawyers and judges hearing accusations against him of malpractice when he cannot defend himself, for he has forgotten his patient's name, doesn't know if he is married and cannot deny that he fell asleep on various occasions in the consulting room. A Kafkaesque world. (1973, p. 99f)

One has to come a long way since Freud, or better stated, one has to travel a considerably more difficult path if we are to treat patients who bring psychotic-like material into our offices. Put differently, we may achieve the states Freud suggests if we can keep the madness out. But that, unfortunately, is a sure dead end for the treatment of many people. Instead, we must learn how to let the madness in (Schwartz-Salant 1993). Bion's "sharks" can represent psychotic material as it attacks and fragments an analysis.

I believe that we can best approach such issues if we allow the field between analyst and analysand to be the analytic object. Then, the analyst's attention attempts to hover within the analytic space; attention is not suspended evenly over the contents of discourse, or over the analysand's or the analyst's inner world, but on the field itself.

Example One

A male analysand, age fifty-seven, a stockbroker, was unable to become disciplined in the market. He had ability and intelligence, and yet he barely subsisted. His character had the cohesiveness to be narcissistically structured by idealization, yet this transference paradigm became shattered over and over again by his failures in the market. When I saw him, he was usually disillusioned, anxious, withdrawn, and despairing. In such states, he would tell me about his difficulties, and it would be impossible for me to listen carefully for more than a minute at a time; my attention invariably fragmented. Yet when I regained it and recalled what he had said, it was clear that had I read his communication as a typescript my attention would not have wandered. It was quite clear, yet the affective field he communicated shrouded it in fragmentation and boredom.

At the beginning of one particular session, I allowed my attention to hover within the space between us and after a few moments the image that we were in a violent storm came into my mind's eye. I focused on this image throughout the session, and the result was that everything he said was easy to listen to and empathize with. The storminess was clearly related to his envy and intense anxieties, yet to interpret them would not have been helpful. Seeing the storm had a containing influence for me and, through me, I think, for him as well. At times during this session, I reflected aloud upon his life as a terrible struggle of surviving storm after storm. He ended the session telling me about a trade he had successfully made and how hopeful he was about a new system he was planning to implement. This felt like an unconscious communication to me that he felt more contained and hopeful—that he was acknowledging a new beginning.

Example Two

This example concerns a woman with whom I had already established the existence of a strong psychotic part. I had managed, at times, to perceive her psychotic part violently attacking her or else helped her see her inner distress as a result of her own pent-up fury and paranoid process. But there was still a lack of any container for this part. Then I attempted, with great effort, to focus upon the field between us, even though my attention tended to fragment. She began speaking about her boyfriend and things he did that caused her concern. After she finished, characteristically, she asked if her worries were crazy. Even though the allusion to the transference was clear, I did not focus on it; instead I explained that I found her thinking to be clear but did not know why so much anxiety and fragmentation went with it. Throughout this, maintaining attention on the field between us was like being in a fog and getting lost here and there. Still, I could attend to her process with some consistency. The sense of fog between us remained until she told me a dream she had had of a man who, to her surprise, was able to control her mother, who, in actuality, could be psychotic. Again, noting but not interpreting the transference, at this point something new became plausible: the field between us was dominated by her mother's psychosis. She had incorporated this psychotic process, and it lived within her as an alien factor. It also dominated the field between us. If I tried to listen to her words, this madness fragmented my thinking and her own, as would have any interpretation. Attending to the field as object seemed to help; she ended the session in a way that was unusual for her, speaking about strengths she knew she had.

I mention these brief examples to illustrate what I mean by attending to the field as an object. The field between two people will usually, at the outset, be felt as empty, like a modern scientific notion of space. If the analyst attends to the interactive field as the object, which means he or she has the courage to carry out this seemingly absurd act—imagining into empty space and assuming something may be there—the analyst may find that the analysand's communications gain a more cohesive form than it was previously possible to achieve. The space will often cease to feel empty. It is not that demons and monsters or any clear image necessarily appears, but often instead a sense of texture and fullness, or one of fragmentation and torn fabric, can be known. Clearly, these are only two of endless possible metaphors for the interactive space.

There may be resistance to the act of perceiving the field as object because the space often feels unsafe. For example, it can lead to states of intimacy that are frightening. Beyond that, one also opens to the impact of projections that are unintegrated and alien to the analysand.[6] This is especially the case when the analysand has been an incest or physical abuse victim. But it can also follow from states of strong and persistent projection from a parental figure. Such abuse or projection can create areas through which the person is subject to overwhelming archetypal processes from within and suggestions from without. Also, states of parental madness are often incorporated (not internalized through introjection, but psychically swallowed), and these have a way of manifesting in the interactive field. Such material, along with deep issues of rage and psychopathy that accompany it, threatens to emerge within the field. I think it is the reality of this process that is especially frightening and can result in countertransference resistance to approaching the field as a "third area" with its own autonomy, which is to say, focusing on it in an embodied way that renders it especially alive and real.

Psychotic Areas Affecting the Analytical Field

When psychotic process is constellated, it is extremely difficult to focus on the field as the analytic object. Bion's "sharks" are attacking. It is not that the field is absent; like the psychotic or mad area itself, it is not contained and has no working or workable structures or image. The experience of this kind of field is dominated by broken links, extreme affects (notably deadness), and by meaninglessness. Although by no means always possible, if, when finding oneself faced with such a field, one can process the material through projective identification, interpretation can have a containing effect through the structure of understanding. The field itself reflects this structure by becoming amenable to focus as the analytic object. The following is such an example.

Example Three

An analysand enters my consultation room and throws down her purse and briefcase. She quickly walks to a corner of the room and sits on the floor. As I look at her, I sense I had better say something or she will explode, screaming, "Why are you just sitting there, do something!" I feel unnerved by this possibility (which has occurred in the past), and I try to hold my ground and wait until I can perceive something more spontaneous and pertinent to the moment. But I lose containment for a moment and begin to combat her intense despair and self-pity over losing her job with an exhortation that she not act out her hysteria. Yet I, too, have become hysterical, for the moment. The air is tense, an atmosphere of no felt containment pervades. Then I begin to reflect upon my feelings. I want to get rid of her. I want her to stop asking me to fix her life. I want her to get well and become more optimistic. It is clear that I have become her mother. At that instant, she says, "You're just like my mother," and I reply, "That is what is being created here, a situation in which you are not contained and are treated as a terrible problem." By virtue of having processed the projective identification (of her mother image), it was possible to say this, and the result was a radical change in the environment. She was no longer overwhelmed, nor was I. She sat down and the session progressed without her acting out or me acting in.

In this case, this session initiated us into work upon her psychotic part. Having never engaged it before, the interpretation through projective identification was necessary to establish some way of approaching the disturbed field. As a consequence, it was possible to imaginally perceive a "front-back" split in the analysand, with a strong component of a split-off exhibitionism. As this could, over the next months, be contained, largely as a result of being portrayed in painting by the analysand, and its presence felt, the level of psychotic fragmentation diminished.

By focusing on the field as the analytic object, one can gain both a sense of containment and the imagination or perception that may not otherwise be available. The nature of psychotic transference and countertransference, ever so subtly acting behind the scenes, falls into view, as does the "front-back" split that often tends to hide it. In the same fashion, one can become sensitized to the existence of the other major splits that generally exist, the vertical splits that characterize dissociation and the horizontal splits that characterize repression, notably mind-body splitting. The awareness of these splits and their mutual interaction is something that our focus on the field creates. This is a great gain in analytic work. Without it, one can stay with one of these splits, known, for example, through projective identification, and never gather up all of the dimensions involved. But the field, experienced as the analytic object, is in a way the Fourth that contains these three fundamental axes of splitting. Unless the opposites are combined along these various "fault lines," there can be no change in internal structure. The idea of an interactive field is especially useful to focus upon this task.

The next example is one in which psychotic material, especially deeply disturbing states of deadness and meaninglessness which covered paranoid levels of envy and rage, was worked on and interpreted many times together. Even though the material was extremely difficult and created an intensely disturbed field that was characterized by broken connections, an alliance existed that allowed our focus to remain exclusively on the field, with the result that we were able to shift toward experiencing the field's dynamics as distinct from what we previously apprehended as "attacks on linking."

Example Four

An analysand, dealing with a severe early abandonment trauma, needed to speak with me on the weekend, but the plans we made for her to do so had to be altered, leading her to a state of anxiety and confusion. When I finally did meet with her, she explained not having called me in the following way:

> Maybe I feel I only take what I get and have no right to anything else. It's like I live with the various pieces and nothing in between. I live going from piece to piece and never ask about what's in between. To do so is

too threatening. I may lose what I already have. I have no sense of what links one state to another, I just hold on, like islands in a sea, each fragile until a next appears, but I have no way of getting from one to the other. Its frightening to think of how they connect for if I want to know anything I can lose what I have. Each state is a potential catastrophe.

When she said these things, I felt attacked and distanced from her. I had dealt with such feelings with her for many months during which she could become conscious of her desire to attack the connection between us because she experienced her needs as absolutely terrifying. When she touched this level in herself, psychotic anxieties emerged that led to numerous acting-out behaviors to quell the pain. But I felt now that interpreting these feelings would only attack her; they would only go over ground she knew so very well. Instead, focusing on the extremely fragmented field between us, it became clear that what I perceived as an attack could be seen as an exteriorization of the chaotic image of the analysand's privation of an inner fabric of connectiveness.

Severe trauma causes loss of an inner sense of a connective fabric. This is felt as an absence, as a privation as in the *privatio boni* view of evil. The absence is felt as evil, as a danger to one's soul. Something that is essential to life is absent, and while the analyst providing some of it may be seen as evoking envy or an attack on linking, such "attacks" can also be seen as an exteriorization of an inner landscape that is broken. To repair it, the person desperately clings to something that was or was not said. He or she does not dare check out its validity; to do so implies trust in the process of getting from one memory to another. But such trust in connectiveness does not exist. Also, to ask anything about what one thinks is real is to risk losing it. The analysand is threatened with being told he or she is crazy or has somehow got it wrong. The other person is invested with knowing the "rules of the game" while the analysand does not.

By focusing on the field and recognizing how persecuted the analysand was by its fragmented state, it became possible to maintain a heart-centered relation to her amid such fragmentation. This was something hard won between us, and interpreting the interaction between us would have blocked its possibility. Instead, she was gradually able to reach out when she was in need, a situation that she had been unable to risk since the severely traumatic events of her infancy.

While we had previously worked on those areas of her madness that were dominated by extremely attacking energies, we had not been able to connect them to split-off attacking feelings toward her mother. Her early history and family structure did not allow for such a thought. It was literally unthinkable. But I believe that work with the field as object gradually allowed this crucial historical link to be made in ways that we could not achieve by interpretation through projective identification processes. A sense of containment emerged through the field that allowed for extremely negative affects to emerge in the transference and to be readily linked to her maternal experience.

The birth of a heart-connection is really the key to field experiences. It creates a sense of safety where none had been known before. Furthermore, when one can also relate to the field in an embodied way, memories hidden in the body can appear while the recollection of such memories was not possible through the psychic unconscious.

The Field as Known Through the
Psychic and Somatic Unconscious

One gets different kinds of information about the psyche, depending on the point of reference from which one is working. Through the psychic unconscious one can perceive disordering parts of the analysand's psyche as they affect the ego, thinking, and the cohesiveness of the analytical process.

The somatic unconscious is the name Jung gave to the subtle body. Jung's model is quite elegant: if you conceive of a conscious-unconscious relationship, then this connection may gather information and experiences along a spectrum running from spirit to matter. As one reaches toward spirit, consciousness fades, as it does also when one approaches matter (Jung 1988, pp. 441ff). Yet, there are distinct experiences of the unconscious along the way. As one moves toward the mental-spiritual level, more toward one's head, the unconscious experienced is the psychic unconscious. Images, patterns, causality, meanings, and history can all fall into one's consciousness. But as one moves toward the body, the conscious/unconscious connection changes. Now one can begin to know what it means to be embodied.

To be embodied is not an easy or obvious act. The mind-body splitting of someone we may be with, or that person's dissociated areas, tends to drive us out of our own embodied state. By being embodied, I mean a particular state of mind in which a person experiences his or her body in a particular way. First one becomes conscious of one's body in the sense of becoming aware of its size. Along with this, one has a particular experience of living in it, which is to say, one feels confined in the space of the body. When this is accomplished, a state that requires that the breath flow freely and is felt as a wave moving up and down the body, one begins to feel that one inhabits the body. In this state the body is a container and one feels one's age. This condition of being embodied is an experience of a medium that exists between what one thinks of as a material body and the mind. This medium is what the alchemists called Mercurius, what others have known by such names as the astral body, the subtle body, and the Kaballistic Yesod (Jung 1955, par. 635), and what Jung called the somatic unconscious (1988, pp. 441ff). To be embodied is to experience this level which is both physical and mental. This is an example of the medium once known as the ether, and in ancient times and especially at the hands of Renaissance alchemists and magicians, it was said to be a substance felt within the human body but also flowing throughout space and forming the pathways along which the imagination and Eros flowed. The ether is probably the qualitative forerunner of the field concept.

To be embodied is an experience of the subtle body. Every complex can be said to have a body, a subtle body. When a complex constellates, its body—to one degree or another—takes over the body of the ego. A male analysand was unusually spirited and clear at the outset of a session and stated metaphorically, "Today I woke up in my own house." He went on to explain that usually he awakes "in his mother's house." This was an expression of losing his own body awareness and instead being in his mother's body image, or that body image constructed by their interactions in childhood. When he awoke "in his own house," in his own body, he felt certain business problems in his life as issues simply to attend to; when he awoke "in his mother's house," these same problems were felt to be overwhelming and persecutory. His behavior would then take on an as-if quality, in sharp distinction to the clarity and strength he manifested when he was "in his own house."

The body of the complex has to be dissolved. This idea—which on the level of the psychic unconscious would be one of dealing with negative introjects that distort authenticity—is carried in alchemical literature by the phrase "destroy the bodies." For example, the *Turba* says: "Take the old black spirit and destroy and torture with it the bodies, until they are changed" (Jung 1955, par. 494). The "old black spirit" is often the person's rage, shame, and paranoia that has been split off from awareness in the first year of life and drives the person out of the body. Making contact with such powerful affects, felt as catastrophic to life itself, is often the only way to "destroy the bodies," to cease living in body images that carry alien qualities that block life.

The somatic unconscious experiences the same material as the psychic unconscious but in terms of body states. These two ways are complementary; a great deal of integration of difficult material that has been taken in from environmental sources can be apprehended through the experience of body states that affect the nature of the interactive field, in ways that cannot be so readily seen through the psychic unconscious.

The psychic unconscious provides us with the *prima materia* of our mental and spiritual processes. These necessarily bring order and logos which, by nature, parcel up the unified whole in order for our consciousness to grasp understanding. We cannot begin to identify or understand anything without our thinking and its concomitant separating and partitioning effects. By referring to the somatic unconscious, we may temporarily lose the structure and order of our mental gains, but we can restore the sense and truth inherent in the psycho-physical totality of an event or an experience. In this way, one can revive the awareness of the interplay and constant flux between the mind/spirit and the soma, which is essential to reestablishing a living experience of the field itself.

Psychotic material impacts on one's consciousness as if it were attacking with sensations or pieces that have no meaning and order. Bion designated such material as "beta products," and he developed a theory of "embryonic thought which forms a link between sense impressions and consciousness" (Meltzer 1973, p. 49). The problem of linking these domains was the focus of much prescientific speculation in the theory of magic and its philosophical underpinning in Stoic thought. But the theory of magic approaches it differently: rather than a theory of thinking, such practitioners focus on a theory of the imagination. In a grand vision of communication on all levels of reality, magicians envisioned a subtle body of links through fantasy, linking fibers known as *vinculum* or sometimes referred to as pneuma, that connected body and mind, people, and (depending on the author) levels reaching toward planetary realms and beyond. In both this theory and Bion's, the imagination is the linking agent, for the soul's language is imagery. And most important, there is an organ that operates as a central station which orients the process of transmuting sense impressions into consciousness. That organ is the heart in human beings and the sun in the Cosmos. The heart is a "cardiac synthesizer," what Aristotle called the hegemonic principle (Couliano 1987, p. 9).

From the point of view of this approach, one could work on the issues of creating links and images to deal with psychotic states through the somatic unconscious. The analyst's inner, imaginal linking of opposites, which is felt as an element of *relation* within the field, would interweave with the analysand's less textured and connected fabric, with sets of broken *relations*. As a consequence, one might be working in this "animistic" way, which goes back to the ancient tradition of magic, on the same issues that more modern theories such as Bion's attempt to address. But here the center is the heart as the organ of thought, not the mind. Through the somatic unconscious, one actually feels a linking current between self and other, a current that has its own heart-centered vision. To illustrate the field and perceptions that emerge from the somatic unconscious, consider the following material.

Example Five

A woman with whom a considerable amount of work on our mutual field had taken place, generally from the point of view of the psychic unconscious, was to have minor surgery. The way she spoke about her body was remarkable to me. No matter what organic condition she was describing, I had a clear sense of contact with her. There was no splitting and beyond this there was a distinct sense that her body was good. This "goodness" was palpable. I felt like a physician, able to talk about any body function or organ with complete openness. What was unusual here was how this state was so clear that it forced itself on my mind rather than allowing me to take it for granted.

But when she spoke about sexuality in any way, or if sexuality was present in her dream material, this body sense vanished. It was as if there was now another body. The sense of the space or field between us radically altered. Now it became diminished in energy, dark and dull in feeling, and with no linking quality at all. The only connection this state had to previous ones had to do with a state of dullness and deadness that she associated to me, thinking them to be only mine. Under the impact of the split opposites in her psychotic part, this was how I felt to her and to myself. But when we eventually dealt with her schizoid states and terror and humiliation over feeling such ego-weakness, it became clear that the deadness she felt in me (which I no longer felt at this stage of our work) was the way she experienced her mother at numerous times in early childhood.

Now this state of deadness was not in me but a quality of the field between us. She could recognize it and could see that it was as if her body had changed. That is how it felt: she had two bodies, one of flesh and another that manifested in dark and disordering ways when any libidinal issues appeared. It was as if her subtle body was possessed by some dark spirit.

She then had a remarkable dream. She dreamed that she was wearing a dark and old nightgown and that she had to get up and begin her day's work. But she could not get the garment off. No matter how much she tried it stuck to her. She thought of taking a shower but she knew that would only make it heavier. The only way she could stop what felt like torture was to wake herself up out of the dream.

The terrible state in the dream was gradually clarified. Rather than understanding this image of the nightgown as, for example, the analysand's shadow, an embodied focus on the field revealed a different view: the garment was her mother's body image which carried madness, depression, and despair over (her mother) having been an incest victim. She had consistently forced the analysand to identify with her throughout her life. For example, the analysand remembered how her mother would tell her that the two of them were alike in that they did not like men. The analysand knew this was not true but, out of fear of her mother's unpredictable violence, said nothing and even agreed at times. There were numerous examples of such direct and enforced projections. Throughout, the analysand was unable to say no to these, for they were the only form of contact she had with her mother, and she also deeply feared her mother's rage if she dared to separate from her. And so she literally wore her mother's madness as a kind of body in which she felt as if she were fused with her mother's body. When this body was enlivened, there was no way of contacting her at all.

It was because we had worked with the psychic unconscious and had established her psychotic sector and a sense of mental-spiritual self that it became possible to access this material. But it was only through becoming aware of the somatic unconscious and of her "two bodies" that she could begin to take action to separate from the ego-alien factors that her mother's madness represented. She could recognize how this body state changed the field between us. I could be embodied with her now and feel the death and darkness that pervaded the field we occupied. And so could she. Only the body allows for a direct experience in this way. As Jung noted, we experience the unconscious through the subtle body in more direct ways, far more tangible than through the psychic unconscious.

As a consequence of this work she eventually was able to reject her mother's projections, while experiencing how frightened she was of daring to accomplish this separation. This was an astonishing act for her, and it was part of her eventually successful labor of taking off her mother's garment of shame and madness. This form of the subtle body also began to diminish in the field between us.

Shared, Unexpected Imagery Within the Interactive Field

When one enters into the field, felt as a space both analyst and analysand occupy, one sometimes discovers totally unexpected imagery. The following example illustrates such material. I choose it because of the seemingly infantile nature of the material, which, in fact, pointed to patterns that could not be usefully reduced to issues of infant development.

Example Six

I had been working with a thirty-four-year old man when we finally began to apprehend material that had an extremely fragmenting effect on his and my own consciousness. When he would speak of his experiences with a woman with whom he was involved, my attention quickly would fragment. He would become schizoid and disembodied.

At the point of this case I want to examine, we were able to have moments of embodiment together in which we felt linked to each other yet also had a sense of being separate, the *coniunctio* rhythm which I discussed in the introduction to this paper. Also, in Winnicott's sense we could each feel alone with the other. But whenever the analysand would mention the woman he was seeing at the time, the field experience between us fragmented. The sense of the space changed texture from rich strands of Eros to being more murky and fractured. We both noticed an atmosphere of fear and paranoid elements that seemed to drive us out of an embodied level. During one session, I pointed this out and he asked, "Where is this fear?" I replied, "In both of us," for I had no true way of seeing it as a projective identification phenomenon. I could have constructed an interpretation from feelings of abandonment I experienced when he fragmented. We had done considerable work of interpretation on such psychotic areas and had understood them as related both to how he experienced his father and ways that his father probably experienced him in the family romance. But to do this again felt stale. There was now too small a container while previously it had been useful.

He raised the question of what could contain these feelings. Jung's assertion that the archetype is the container came to mind. Certainly we could together reflect on a son-lover myth as structuring the space between us, and there are numerous other images to choose from, for example, the myth in alchemy of the son swallowed by the dragon, which then cuts him up into thousands of parts. I noted that such a powerful image might be organizing our interaction. Saying this changed the field: we both felt more in control and far less fragmented. We could then gain some sense of understanding and relatedness, but there was little soul to the experience between us, and embodiment in any depth was not possible. Archetypal amplifications, like developmental understanding, could create a mental-spiritual kind of order, a discovery of spirit but not of soul. Such interpretations would not allow for a field of attachment that alone could perhaps create the bridges necessary for helping him leave the magnetic sphere of the son-lover field without heroically repressing it and, by necessity, losing his body awareness.

In the next session, he began associating to the previous day. It was not difficult to feel embodied, and I managed to see a vague presence of a child. I asked him how old he felt during the events he was relating, and he replied that he felt five or six and the feeling clearly reminded him of leaving his mother.

Remaining in an embodied state, with a slightly lowered level of attention, I then experienced an image appearing that pointed to a far younger age. While remaining embodied, at three different times the image of what seemed to be an infant sucking a maternal breast, with the nipple clearly the infant's object, pressed upward into my awareness. After some hesitation I mentioned the image to him. I must emphasize that this kind of intervention is prompted by what are felt as the dynamics of the shared field. In a sense, one allows the field to have an imaginal autonomy.

Continuing to stay embodied, with both of us feeling this state of separation yet also connection within a textured feeling of space, the image changed: no longer an infant at the breast, now the image was only of a mouth and nipple. It felt enlivened, as if it were a "third thing" that in some sense we both shared. I recalled that at the beginning of the session he had given me some references he thought I wanted, and I now told him that my taking them was like taking his nipple into my mouth. We both sat with the mouth-nipple image. It could not be reduced to the infant-breast couple nor, as he mentioned and I agreed, to mouth-penis or anus-penis, but was something else. The image of a mouth grasping a nipple seemed to have its own field and meaning.

He asked me how old I felt now, and I felt my actual age, as did he at this time. Yet we still had the seemingly early-maternal image of the mouth and nipple with us. This was perplexing. It seemed so clearly to beg for some understanding in terms of his or my own early breast experiences, or in terms of archetypal images such as the "male mother," yet this violated the experience. There was a sense of the ineffable, not any powerful archetypal level but rather something more subtle, yet clearly Other. Staying in intimate contact in this way for several minutes, he then said that this experience reminded him of an image of being knighted. He said he imagined a young knight on his knees receiving a sword from an older knight. Within this, he said, there was a sense of being empowered and a sense of the transmission of power.

How could something so obviously referring to infancy as a mouth-nipple image be anything else? Yet, I came to recognize that this is the essential mystery of work with interactive fields. When they open to an archetypal dimension, the field may make use of imagery in which we could each be a nipple or mouth to the other. Yet, rather than being a replay of infant dynamics, something else is indicated. There is a field of linkages, felt as a texture that appears to open to other archetypal images, here those of male initiation.

Summary

This paper defines and gives examples of the *interactive field*, a "third area" that partakes of both the objective properties of the collective unconscious and the combined subjectivities of analyst and analysand. It explores the dynamics of this field, especially noting the fundamental rhythm of union states and a resultant disorder, the alchemical *nigredo*. Generally, as with Jung's work on the transference, alchemical symbolism has been the guide, for that body of thought was primarily concerned with the transformation of form. This issue is addressed by the interactive field concept, which in turn is related in two ways: through a psychic and a somatic unconscious. The role of embodiment is emphasized as the way of experiencing the somatic unconscious and the play of affects, structure, and energy in the field.

In addressing the nature of the space in which analysis occurs, there is no intention to denigrate the more direct interpretive or empathic dimension of analytic work that may not explicitly focus on a field between people. Both approaches are necessary: each complements the other. In a sense, the field is like the ground against which projective and introjective or empathic process is played out, but at times focusing on the field itself rather than the dynamic processes between analyst and analysand has particular value. It can be a way of containing psychotic elements, and it can also allow for an increased consciousness without explicit interpretation. Most important, experiencing the field can facilitate a transformation of internal structure.

The interactive field idea has been used here as the analytic object. Examples demonstrate how this opens to the awareness and experience of a space with its own processes not identical to the combined projections of analyst and analysand. The field, as such, is beyond the three-dimensional notion of container-contained focused on the projective and introjective processes of the individuals involved. There may be some grounds for stating that the field approach, conceived of as an imaginal reality with its own autonomy, is akin to a fourth dimension that complements the more usual three-dimensional model of analysis.

Notes

1. See Ogden, p. 62f., n. 1, for further references.

2. In Jung's study of the transference (1946), he employed alchemical imagery to understand the interaction between analyst and analysand. His structural analysis of the transference was based on a quaternity of elements comprising the conscious position of both people, and their unconscious, contrasexual components. This model can be extended to two subjective positions and the unconscious of each person, but the use of the contrasexual components, anima and animus, to represent the collective unconscious

is of particular significance for a field concept. For anima and animus are, in essence, *in between* structures, mediators between conscious and unconscious. This, along with the fact that subjectivities of two people are involved, is an element that gives the status of Jung's structural analysis a field quality that is *in between* the realm of subjectivity and objectivity.

Jung regarded his analysis of the transference as focused on its archetypal nature, and he also believed that the unconscious combinations of the psyches of analyst and analysand were to be uncoupled through an analysis of the analysand's projections. Consequently, the "third area," which Jung beautifully explicates through alchemical symbolism, is ultimately used as a source of information about the analysand's projections. The field's underlying dynamics, *per se*, are not regarded as useful or worth experiencing in their own right, even though Jung's frequent quotations of alchemical authors also shows that he definitely had this possibility in mind.

But Jung's analysis became skewed, and I believe undermined, by his aversion to one important stage on the way toward the alchemical goal, the lapis or Philosopher's Stone. This stage is the hermaphrodite, the tenth woodcut of the *Rosarium Philosophorum*. Jung regarded it as a monstrosity and as the result of the alchemist's failure to understand the process of projection. He saw it as a crude creation that ultimately came out of a process totally bogged down in sexuality. He was quick also to condemn Freud for this same "failure." As a consequence of this negative result, in Jung's view, he was left with an interpretation of the alchemical material that underplayed the very alchemical imagery he has so carefully explicated, while insisting on seeing the mutual creation of analyst and analysand as a result of projection. That is, the active, inexhaustible nature of the collective unconscious is all but neglected; it is not treated as a field that is constellated in the transference/countertransference process. Another side effect of Jung's attitude is that he was led to consider the alchemical imagery itself as pertinent to masculine psychology. In other places, I have dealt with these issues more fully, noting that, by undervaluing the hermaphrodite as a viable "third thing" with its own mystery, Jung has essentially limited the value of his analysis of the transference (1984). One may accept Jung's great caution about the dangers of "sexualizing" the contents of the unconscious and all forms of literalization. But we must also recognize that his pioneering effort has shortcomings, including the manner in which he divides personal and archetypal aspects of the transference. These nearly always intertwine.

Nevertheless, whatever value lies in the idea of an interactive field is heavily indebted to Jung's study. It has been noted that his quaternity model has the same structure as energy diagrams in physics. These indicate a remarkable quality of information transfer between molecules that are not in contact with one another. Various energy levels in one molecule may change and induce changes in another. The suggestion from this remarkable parallel is that changes in the analyst's unconscious, for example, have an affect not only on the conscious of the analysand, but on the unconscious as well (Popp). One finds the same awareness four hundred years earlier in the alchemical text *Splendor Solis*, in which seemingly separable states affect one another in the same (sixfold) pattern of information transfer (McLean 1981, p. 83f).

Jung's analysis contains all of this, *in potentia* if not actually, and in turn it is a model of the interactive field, composed of mutual subjectivities and the objective level of the psyche. In a sense, there are two strands in his study, one an alchemical amplification and the other a psychological interpretation of it. I regard my formulation as being true to Jung's amplifications and reflections on the alchemical imagery he employed, and more separate from the manner in which he interpreted the alchemical material in terms of the analysis of projections.

3. The differentiation of opposites into successive aspects of a process, on the one hand, and as two different "things" on the other, is ancient and goes back to the pre-Socratic philosopher Heraclitus (Kirk and Raven, pp. 189-190).

4. Jung has discussed such a process of "conscious projection" (1988, pp. 1495-

1496), and Corbin has noted it in the Sufi notion of *himma* (1969, pp. 220f). The result of this conscious sacrifice (of interpretation) and imaginal thrust is that the quality of the field, the third thing, perceptively and palpably changes. One can become aware of the texture of the surrounding space. The exact quality of change is as difficult to describe as the feeling of inspiration that is often present, and in fact it is similar, including an enlivening of the senses. Color and detail become more vivid; even the taste in the mouth can change. There is a bit of an adrenalin rush, or in spiritual terms, one could say one senses the presence of divinity.

　　5. This paradoxical nature of the interactive field is analogous to the alchemical container, the *vas hermeticum*. See Rosen's paper "Pouring Old Wine into a New Bottle," in this volume.

　　6. In his lectures on Nietzsche, Jung speaks of projections as being a subtle form of matter, carrying weight and actually capable of lodging in the spinal cord (1988, p. 1495).

References

Corbin, H. 1969. *Creative Imagination in the Sufism of Ibn Irabi.* Ralph Manheim, trans. Princeton, N.J.: Princeton University Press.

Couliano, Ioan. 1987. *Eros and Magic in the Renaissance.* Chicago: University of Chicago Press.

Fordham, Michael. 1957. Notes on the transference. In T*echnique in Jungian Analysis*, Library of Analytical Psychology, Vol. 2. London: Heinemann.

Freud, S. 1912. Recommendations to physicians practising psycho-analysis. In *Standard Edition*, vol. 12. London: Hogarth, 1955.

Green, Andre. 1975. The analyst, symbolization and absence in the analytic setting. *International Journal of Psycho-Analysis* 56/1.

Jung, C. G. 1944. *Psychology and Alchemy. CW*, vol. 12. Princeton, N.J.: Princeton University Press, Second edition, 1968.

――. 1946. Psychology of the transference. In *CW* 16: 163–326. Princeton, N.J.: Princeton University Press, 1954.

――. 1955. *Mysterium Coniunctionis. CW*, vol. 14. Princeton, N.J.: Princeton University Press, 1963.

――. 1988. *Nietzsche's Zarathustra*, vols. 1 and 2. James L. Jarrett, ed. Princeton, N.J.: Princeton University Press.

Kirk, G. S., and J. E. Raven. 1969. *The Pre-Socratic Philosophers.*Cambridge: Cambridge University Press.

McLean, Adam, ed. 1980. *Rosarium Philosophorum.* Edinburgh: Magnum Opus Sourceworks.

――. 1981. *Splendor Solis.* Edinburgh: Magnum Opus Sourceworks.

Meltzer, Donald. 1973. *The Kleinian Development, Part III: The Clinical Significance of the Work of Bion.* Perthshire, England: Clunie Press.

Ogden, Thomas. 1994. *Subjects of Analysis.* Northvale, N.J.: Jason Aronson.

Popp, C. Psychic energy in the analytic relationship. Unpublished manuscript.

Racker, Heinrich. 1968. *Transference and Countertransference.* New York: International Universities Press.

Schwartz-Salant, N. 1984. Archetypal factors underlying sexual acting-out in the transference/countertransference process. In *Transference/Countertransference,* N. Schwartz-Salant and M. Stein, eds. Wilmette, Ill.: Chiron Publications.

――. 1989. *The Borderline Personality: Vision and Healing.* Wilmette, Ill.: Chiron Publications.

――. 1991. Vision, interpretation and the interactive field. *Journal of Analytical Psychology*, 36, n. 3, pp. 343–366.

――. 1991b. Anima and animus in Jung's alchemical mirror. *Chiron: Anima and Animus in Clinical Practice.* Wilmette, Ill.: Chiron Publications.

————. 1993. Jung, madness and sexuality: reflections on psychotic transference and countertransference. In *Mad Parts of Sane People in Analysis*, M. Stein, ed. Wilmette, Ill.: Chiron Publications.

Sheldrake, Rupert. 1991. *The Rebirth of Nature*. New York: Bantam Books.

Stolorow, R., B. Brandchaft, and G. Atwood. 1987. *Psychoanalytic Treatment: An Intersubjective Approach*. Hillsdale, N.J.: Analytic Press.

von Franz, Marie-Louise. 1974. *Number and Time*. Evanston, Ill.: Northwestern University Press.

————. 1980. *On Divination and Synchronicity*. Toronto: Inner City Books.

Winnicott, D. W. 1971. *Playing and Reality*. New York: Basic Books.

A Concept of Participation

Verena Kast

translated by Douglas Whitcher

In the deepest sense we all dream not out of ourselves but out of what lies between us and the other.

C. G. Jung to James Kirsch, *Letters*, vol. 1

Introduction

Transformation in therapy can be seen in turning points marked by new symbols that rise up out of the analytic vessel. These symbols may bring with them a new attitude toward life or make it possible to differentiate among several deep-seated feelings that have become mixed and clouded.

Symbols are activated in therapeutic relationships when analysts devote interest to the entire personality of their analysands, including their unique facets, potentials, and inhibitions. This interest

Verena Kast is a professor of psychology at the University of Zurich and a training analyst and lecturer at the C. G. Jung Institute of Zurich. She lectures throughout the world and is the author of numerous books on psychological issues, including *The Dynamics of Symbols, Fundamentals of Jungian Psychology, Imagination as Space of Freedom, Growth through Emotions, Interpretations of Fairy Tales, The Nature of Loving,* and *The Creative Leap.*

37

generally animates the unconscious and results in the perception of symbols that are found to have meaning. These symbols must be worked on, given form, and interpreted.

The goal of therapy is to take up those starts of growth that bud in the psyche. We then come to understand ourselves better, including our darker sides, the projection of which becomes easier to identify. The overall goal is to become more autonomous, more open to relationship, and more honest, so that we can deal with ourselves and others with greater competence.

Activation of the unconscious takes place in an analytical relationship. This intimate relationship, a meeting in which each person always has more to learn from the other, is a highly focused encounter through which new facets of ourselves spring to life and become grafted into our being. One difference between the analytical relationship and a nonprofessional relationship is the great amount of attention devoted to the phenomenon of transference and countertransference.

In 1929, Jung added the term *countertransference* to the working vocabulary of psychotherapy. In 1946, he published "The Psychology of the Transference," which remains in my opinion the single most complete theory of transference, countertransference, and relationship.

My diagram of transference and countertransference (opposite page) is based on Jung's, which was based on an alchemical text. One relationship takes place between the ego of the analyst and that of the analysand. I would describe this relationship as comprising the entire realm of encounter offered by analysis. Here the analyst is perceived as a real person and approaches the analysand as such. Transference is thought of as the distorted perception of a relationship. Old ways of relating—complexes—are imported into the analytical relationship or transferred onto the analyst. Transference is generally a compromise between the original content of a complex and the defensive structures built up against it. Not only the content of complexes and patterns of relating can be transferred, but also archetypal images.

I think of countertransference as the analyst's emotional response to the analysand, especially when transference is an issue. A mysterious relationship or fusion appears to exist between the unconscious of the analyst and that of the analysand. The concept of the interactive field in therapy is an attempt to describe this fusion. The shared unconscious is sensed as the atmosphere of the

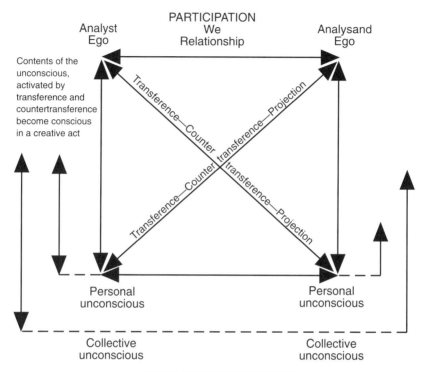

PARTICIPATION
Analyst   We   Analysand
Ego   Relationship   Ego

Contents of the
unconscious,
activated by
transference and
countertransference
become conscious
in a creative act

Transference—Counter transference—Projection

Transference—Counter transference—Projection

Personal   Personal
unconscious   unconscious

Collective   Collective
unconscious   unconscious

PARTICIPATION MYSTIQUE
The shared unconscious "atmosphere" of the relationship
The ground for psychic infection
Countertransference presupposes such an "unconscious relationship"

relationship. It is the ground for psychic "infection," an example of which is the experience the analyst has when she feels in her body the unperceived and unexpressed anxiety of the analysand. "Countertransference" presupposes such an unconscious relationship. At its best, this "communal" unconscious provides the basis by which the analysand can take part in the analyst's self-regulating function, assuming that it is operating. These unconscious processes, which may even allow us to speak of an unconscious identity of two persons, make it possible for constellations of complexes and archetypes to surface in the psyche of the analyst. The analyst may be the one who becomes aware of a constellation and finds an image, personal or archetypal, for the emotions that have been stirring underground.

A central symbolic situation from the life of the analysand may become conscious by means of the analyst's creative act. When this happens, the analysand feels understood. An important emotional experience has been confirmed, understood, and communicated back in such a way that it may contribute significantly to the analysand's enlarged self-understanding, no less than to the grasp of his or her current dilemma (Kast 1990, pp. 180–181).

Interpretation

If we take seriously the notion of an interactive field, we must first of all abandon the idea that one person (the analyst) is the one in the know, whose job it is to teach the analysand. But while swimming together with the analysand in an interactive sea would fulfill our needs for symbiosis—as long as symbols of unity and wholeness are constellated—we would watch ourselves go mercilessly to pieces when issues of boundary and conflict arise. This would cause grandiose suffering. Too little justice would be done to our legitimate needs for greater consciousness, self-understanding, and being understood by someone else, and there would be too little recognition of the fact that here is someone who has asked for help in dealing with a problem in life and who should be permitted the expectation that an analyst is a professional in dealing with interactive processes.

This dilemma of empathic understanding of and relatedness to the in-between space of the analysis on the one hand and the need for clarification and greater consciousness on the other is often misunderstood as a dilemma of technique versus relationship. This is true of psychotherapy as a whole, and especially true of Jungian therapy. It is my thesis that mastery of various techniques allows us to abandon ourselves with greater confidence to the mysteries of the interactive field. It is not a matter of technique against relationship. It is a matter of both. There are moments in therapy in which technique assumes a position of priority and those when mystery is called for with greater urgency.

It seems to me that some techniques do more justice to the interactive field than others, especially techniques employing active imagination. Such interpretive techniques set the stage, making it easier for both parties to step into a common symbolic world of memories, meanings, and emotions. The imagination suggests its own interpretations, not initially proposed by the analyst; these arise out of the relationship of two persons and their orientation to symbols that come their way. (Later I will elaborate on this thesis by describing two cases.)

Technique and Mystery

A group of people answering questionnaires on the topic of "transformation in analysis" made comments about therapeutic technique. They said that changes in analysis have little to do with the technique of the therapist and a lot to do with the relationship. Naturally there is no such thing as an analytic relationship in which no techniques are employed, especially if we understand technique as an activity that liberates natural, inherent energies of the personality. Technique could be defined as the sum of all means and rules that help to locate and realize the creative potentials of the psyche (*techne* in Greek means "art").

Technique is the means to a goal. Our goal is to raise something to consciousness that has been unconscious: repressed memories, emotions, creative potential. Ultimately the goal is to restore the psyche's own tendency for self-regulation. Transformation becomes possible when this tendency becomes real and realizable. It is to technique that we should look in our search for a way to flush out and draw forth the hidden facets of the psyche. Technique lets human difficulties and capacities become known.

Technique is a way of disclosing.   (Heidegger 1978)

Every technique reveals, but each technique conceals as well, obstructing our view of ways that would otherwise be open to us. The greatest danger of technique is the expenditure of energy that it may require: we may go through all the ins and outs without getting to the source and heart of a matter. We may use a technique for its own sake and forget to ask ourselves why we are using it.

For example, we may interpret a dream with great finesse while neglecting the dream's passion; the dream's emotional quality may have led to a very different interpretation. Or we may be so preoccupied with the interpretation of transference and countertransference that we ignore an image hovering before us for a moment only to disappear before we noticed it was there. We see only one part of the person and are distracted by seeing it much too clearly.

The essence of technique in psychotherapy is in the therapeutic relationship. Technique helps us to mold this relationship into a form that holds the highest degree of psychological life. This allows the inner core of the analysand to achieve expression. The therapeutic relationship is affected by all of the techniques we employ.

The Mystery Status

When I ask about the relation between technique, mystery, and transformation in therapy, I am not pitting therapeutic relationship against methods and tools (technique). Rather, I am concerned with locating those techniques that are most apt to disclose something that has been hidden: a surprise enclosed in my own being, something new in the world, an unexpected form of relationship. This creates new factors of influence. After all, it is through our influence on others that we finally come to know ourselves. Influence in relationship is mutual and circular rather than one-way and linear. This involves a great mystery, which reminds me of Eckhardt Wiesenhütter's notion of "mystery status," inspired by the German Romantic poet Novalis. Wiesenhütter suggested that, in addition to marital status, financial status, professional status, and emotional status, we also have a mystery status. Mysteries are revealed and resolved slowly, as the encounter between two persons reaches deeper levels. One person's mystery is enclosed in the other person's being, and one's mysteries are never completely disclosed.

Taking this mystery seriously creates a certain attitude. In therapy, this is an attitude of respect for the encounter that precludes superior or advanced knowledge. Knowledge is gained only with the effort and patience required to climb the many steps that lead to a mystery. In addition, the mystery status implies an attitude of wonder at the many possible roads that people could take, possibilities that always transcend what we think is "humanly possible," for good and bad. We allow a radically open-ended future for each person. Life cannot be pinned in place or reduced to a limited set of pathways that each lead to an outcome already known. Therapists become partners and allies who help analysands feel their way along these unmarked paths. Trust in openness gives the process a chance. The goal of therapy involves respect for the mystery status, according to Wiesenhütter, who describes this goal as the "opening of a person to the possibility of creative becoming" (1969, p. 308).

This is also the goal of therapy as formulated by C. G. Jung: to meet changes in life with the spark of creativity, as if life were a journey. But part of what it means to be creative is to let our fields lie fallow for a time, weather the dry spells, and wait out dead ends. Creative becoming is one goal of therapy; another is to give consent to oneself to grow as a person, which includes all the bumps and bruises that make us who we are (Kast 1990).

If we give priority to the mystery status, we become focused not only on the mystery of one human being, but also on the mystery of the process of transformation in general. This fosters a unique therapeutic attitude, which employs techniques that are continuously adapted and readapted to the individual with the goal of disclosing something of the mystery. As therapists, we disclose it for the sake of the person in therapy and for our own sake. The analysand is no longer simply a collection of complexes, although the complexes remain; the person becomes something more, unfathomable and exciting, and this is what makes transformation possible. The inner activity of transformation may remain invisible and mysterious for long stretches of time. Jung's entire life work consisted of understanding and experimenting with the process of transformation.

Some therapeutic attitudes seem to allow for transformation and personal change better than others. It seems that we can give change a better chance if we create a therapeutic atmosphere that is evocative of the mystery status. In such a climate, changes are less disturbing and more expected. I think it is also important that we attempt to describe processes of transformation that occur in therapy, that we describe them as closely as possible in order to edge our way along toward the central mystery. Among the various factors that make transformation possible, I would like to elaborate on one that I find especially important.

Consent for Mutual Participation as a Condition for the
Restoration of the Psyche's Self-regulating Function

Since techniques are never independent of the therapies in which they are used, I will describe the relationship between technique and mystery by means of a clinical example, after making some preliminary remarks.

For Jung, the psyche was, like the living body, a self-governing system. Jung saw this self-regulating activity above all in the unconscious reactions directed toward the one-sidedness of consciousness. These reactions maintain the integrity of the structure of the psyche while making it possible to transcend a given standpoint (change or transformation).

The self-regulating function of the psyche works through symbols. Symbols are cross-sections of human experience: they condense meaning into microcosmic drops and are the focal points of human development. Symbols display the themes in life that create our difficulties, the very same themes that harbor new prospects. Thus symbols make visible the ways that we can grow. Moreover, they show us that our personal problems are typically human, something that strikes us when we discover the same symbols that we thought were our own private revelations in fairy tales, myths, literature, and works of art.

The fact that symbols have dimensions of both inhibition and development becomes clear when we understand how symbols help us to see complexes. Complexes are constellations of condensed memories, experiences, and fantasies that are attracted to each other on the basis of a given theme and which share a common quality of emotional resonance. Complexes influence our perception of the world, feelings, relationships, and formation of ideas on the one hand, and they also influence somatic processes.

When complexes are touched off in daily life, we "overreact." The emotion bound up with the complex hits us like a strong wave, and fantasies that stem from the situation at the root of a complex distort our perception of the situation of the present moment. We try to get hold of ourselves by deploying stereotypical defense mechanisms.

For example, many people suffer from a complex that has to do with being excluded. This indicates that, in the course of their life, they have repeatedly had the feeling of being ignored and found the experience very painful. They have a hard time being in a situation without asking the question "Am I being slighted?" When such persons are excluded, their emotional reaction sums up all the fantasies and memories they have ever had of being skipped over, distorting their perception of the current situation. Often the defensive strategy is to write off people who exclude them.

The emotion that gives the complex its power contains the energy that the ego complex needs in order to get a handle on this problem. But there is a way to make this energy available: we can let the complex "image itself out" in symbolic shapes and forms.

Thus symbols are the workplaces to which the complexes are invited in the here and now. Symbols give the ego ground on which to stand to confront the complexes. This confrontation has both backward-looking and forward-looking aspects. The symbol affords access both to memory and to expectation. It leads to personal memories of those situations that have left marks and scars, and it shows us the light at the end of the complex's narrow tunnel.

Collusive Transference-Countertransference and the Formation of Symbols

Complexes can appear otherwise than in symbols. They come up in all kinds of relationships, including the therapeutic relationship, where they often create collusive transferences and countertransferences.

The collusion (see Willi 1975) describes a situation in which the behavior of the analyst is determined by a polarization to the behavior of the analysand. Even if the analyst becomes conscious that this polarizing process is taking place, he or she may not be able to stop it right away. A stereotypical pattern of relationship repeats itself again and again. One of Jung's most important definitions of the complex gives us some insight into this:

> It [the complex] obviously arises from the clash between a demand of adaptation and the individual's constitutional inability to meet the challenge. Seen in this light, the complex is a valuable symptom which helps us to diagnose an individual disposition. (1921, par. 926)

We might consider the fact that Jung's "demand of adaptation" is placed by the persons to whom we are closest and on whom we are most dependent. Thus, in the complexes, we may see signs not only of our individual dispositions but also of the histories of our relationships in childhood and later, along with the affects and stereotypical ways of behaving that have become so deeply ingrained.

Childhood histories generally consist of two persons: a parent, friend, sibling, or relation, and the child. In analysis, the complex may divide itself up according to this pattern. The analyst behaves like the parent in some complex-producing situation from the analysand's childhood, and the analysand behaves like the child, or vice versa. Such analytical situations can be described as "complex-laden." They run a typical course, are very emotional, and lead to a dead end. They run up against defensiveness, both from the analyst and the analysand. Both parties feel themselves to be under pressure. They are locked in a transference-countertransference collusion.

I would like to propose the following thesis in regard to this collusion: only when the complex's constellation has been understood and felt as a pattern of relating from childhood is the way clear for the formation of new symbols. Persons who played a part in the past must be experienced as the analysand's own inner figures before the complex can "image itself out." This experience may first become possible by means of the analyst. Complexes that have become lodged in the transference and countertransference may be taken as symbolic forms. These, too, must be emotionally understood, otherwise the energy residing in the complex all too often stays tied up in a somewhat childish transference-countertransference quarrel.

Collusive transferences and countertransferences need to be apprehended. But we may encounter numerous tangles before we wake up to what the situation is doing with us. If episodes are truly met with understanding—which means that analysands gain insight into themselves and their past, and analysts see why they have been behaving the way they have—then new symbolic forms may come within reach. This requires a great deal of empathy with ourselves.

At the heart of each complex is an archetype, according to Jungian theory. Typical complexes have become the subjects of popular conversation: mother complexes, father complexes, power complexes, and so forth. Archetypes are anthropological constants. They are the motifs that run through all human experience, expression, work, and behavior. They give form and shape to the heart of human experience. Archetypal ideas funneled through personal complexes take on a personal coloration. On the one hand, archetypes are structured so that they reach across boundaries of what is considered physical and psychological. Transitional phases of human life, for example, give rise to comparable emotions, fantasies, susceptibility to physical disease, and hopes for salvation. We can thank our complexes for making these anthropological constants kettles of fish of our very own.

Besides this structural aspect, archetypes have an inner dynamic that brings potential things into actuality. Jung described this as a "principle of spontaneous movement and activity." It accounts for the free flow of images that can be evoked from the psyche, as well as for the free hand that is given to the ego complex in fashioning them. The creative impulse builds on this.

If a collective symbol lands in the yard of one's experience, or if one happens to see personal difficulties in the light of a collective symbolic process, there is usually a great commotion. There is hope, the fantasy that there may be a way to cope. It seems that transformation lies within the reach of the possible or has somehow entered the realm of experience. One's emotional palette is noticeably different from before, which opens the door to new ways of doing things. All of Jungian technique focuses on this goal of making it possible for the psyche's self-governing system to bring archetypal images to bear on the ego complex.

Two Clinical Examples of Participation

1. An Unremarkable Man

Complexes have a way of dividing themselves up into roles that are assumed in collusive patterns of transference-countertransference in therapy. This is especially likely when we are working on aspects of parental complexes that are experienced as obstacles. I am of the view that lack of participation in childhood is at the root of what we call negative mother and negative father complexes. Parents did not or could not allow their children to take part to the extent that was needed. Parents and children did not merge in that oceanic feeling of togetherness that would have allowed the children to nest in a secure "we" from which they could then set out on their own.

Thus such children learned to rely on their ego complexes in situations where autonomy was not the issue. An important consequence is that such persons as adults have the feeling that they "do not belong" and are not worthy of love.

A forty-two-year-old man had a father who gave him the feeling that he should always be remarkable. The man experienced his father in childhood as rarely having seen anything good in him; he was very rejecting of his son. "You not only have to like doing things, you also have to be able to do things," he recalled his father saying. Or, "I do everything great; scram, little squirt." The boy would have liked to have heard, "We can do it together."

Beginning with the fifty-first hour, the therapy showed signs of getting stuck. The father complex was constellated. Dreams of father figures were re-experienced using guided fantasy. A letter to father was written, borrowing from Kafka. The father problem became the theme at a psychodrama weekend. The complex-laden figure of his father was projected onto others, including me. I heard the message: "You expect something remarkable from me." I interpreted this as a transference of the situation with his father, who expected something remarkable from him. He understood. Nothing changed.

After a few more hours, I realized that I was beginning to want something from him. It did not have to be remarkable, but I did at least want something to change. I communicated this realization in the following way: "I am getting impatient. I want something to change. But I have no right to demand a change."

"Father never would have said the last part of what you just said," he responded. The complex had clearly become divided up into a collusion. The father part of the complex had been delegated to me, which I had accepted. The child part was left for him. It irritated me that I no longer saw and trusted in his potential for growth the way I usually can. I saw him exactly the way the complex would have it: as a failure. As soon as he was gone, it was easy for me to differentiate between my identification with a part of his complex and my usual attitude.

He then told me that I really did expect something remarkable from him. He felt so small and dumb, so like a little child, that he wanted to bury himself in a ton of bricks. But first he would like to put me on the rack once so I would know how it feels. He wanted so much to change—if only I could think of something.

He was well aware of his rage and sense of impotence. We could both accept this. But nothing happened. He was not remembering any more dreams. I felt increasing pressure to do something. But nothing occurred to me. He became more and more demanding. "I thought you were good. . . ." I ran out of ideas.

In the sixty-third hour, I was less irritated that usual. Suddenly the whole thing seemed comical. What was going on? And then I saw—in a countertransferential image—my analysand as a small and very lonely boy standing in a bleak place, surrounded by a number of tall figures all talking down at him. He shrank and shrank, obviously feeling like a "nothing." I told him about my image and said it described how I had been feeling for the past few hours. Together we reconstructed the little boy's feelings as he crouched beneath these large figures. He called them "giants."

We also dealt with his intense desire for revenge implied by his comment that he would like to see me on the rack before burying himself in a ton of bricks. Now the climate between us had changed. Before, I had had to fight off drowsiness. Now I was wide awake. We were no longer one step removed from each other in battle position. There was a clear sense of "we."

When the analysand came to the next hour, he told me he felt as if he had been reborn. He felt as if he had been able finally to cast off the "armored shell of his father complex." Suddenly he realized that he did not have to play only the part of the small boy. With me, he had played the part of his father, and not only with me. It had been a rough week. He realized how badly he had behaved—worse than his father—and he had been projecting it the whole time! Without noticing it!

I asked him what made him think that he had cast off the armored shell of his father complex. He told me he was no longer acting like a little boy. He no longer felt as if he needed to achieve anything remarkable. It was enough that he had gone through this change. His wife had asked him what had happened to him; he seemed so much younger and happier. He had finally asked his boss for a raise and had gotten it. He dreamed of a man his own age who fascinated him. He must get to know this man, who seemed more decisive and yet more playful than he. During the hour, I felt very relieved, glad that such new vistas could open up. I went back and forth between a sense of hope that the next round of work with this father complex would not begin too soon and a sense of curiosity about what doors might still be open for him.

The transformation described above took place in what I view as a very typical course of events. Before complexes image themselves out, they tend to divide themselves up. The division of roles amounted to a delegation, which I interpreted as soon as I became aware of it. Interpretation always creates distance. I had to become conscious of the other part of the complex—me as a small boy, a "nothing" who strikes out in revenge before his final downfall. I had to give up my resistance against the countertransference by having more empathy with myself. I had to allow myself to be amused, instead of locking myself more fiercely into a position of irritation. Only then did I become open to my unconscious. Only then could I place the image that spoke to both of us into the therapeutic process. This image gave us the experience of being a "we" and put us both in touch with the unconscious. Then the psyche could begin to govern itself again. I was freed of my complex-laden, judgmental straitjacket. The analysand felt as if he had been "reborn," began behaving differently, and brought a new, archetypal symbol into the therapeutic process. The dream of the fascinating, unknown man his own age gave us quite a bit to do in the following hours.

My Thesis

If we are able to restore an original "we" situation, often against considerable resistance from both sides, then we have established the possibility of receiving what the psyche has been sending our way. The psyche begins to regulate itself again. Since the psyche of the analysand had not been governing itself, this function had to be assumed from my side. If we analysts can open the door to our own images in the midst of situations that are emotionally trying, and if these images are really coming from an analytical "we" or from the space "between" rather than from our own complexes, then these images speak to the analysand, become the keys that unlock new fantasies and emotions and new ways of conducting ourselves. It is as if therapy offers the possibility of "standing in" for the other person. The creative impulse comes through to us, and then we send it back later on. But this presupposes that one psyche is really attuned to the other.

The self-regulation of the analysand's psyche can be put into service by means of the therapist. This seems to me a matter of the greatest mystery. It is intimately bound up with the idea of transformation. For me, these are the kinds of situations that give a clear sense of something moving forward. They give me hope for more development and changes.

I think it is also worth noting that I had to use all the techniques at my disposal in order to get out of my identification with one part of the complex. Otherwise I would have been blinded to the mystery of this person. I would have reduced him to a "nothing but" just the way his negative father complex had done. It would have hindered me from believing in transformation by means of anything short of termination.

2. A Woman Without Hands

The analysand was a forty-nine-year-old woman in business, married, with two adult children. Originally, she began analysis because she could not free herself of a deep-seated feeling of emptiness in life, in spite of major success in business. She thought that this feeling of her life as empty and trivial must be a sign that she was having a midlife crisis, that her crisis must have hit somewhat later than normal. She had avoided the unhappiness of the "empty nest syndrome" by burying herself in the business that she had inherited from her father. She appeared confident to me, highly motivated, a bit wiry; dreamy eyes contrasted with her tight face and her nice, modest clothing.

Her feeling of emptiness did not come across right away. At first I felt confused; I had no idea where to begin, and I felt pressured to get right down to business. Taking these feelings as my starting point, I spoke with her about how we might work together. We would be finding out together what life wanted from her. Her dreams and fantasies would be of interest, and we would have to pay careful attention to what was going on between us. I ended my speech by saying that we needn't worry so much about making the grass grow. The grass would grow of its own accord; our job would be to pick the stones out of the field. She responded by assuring me that she would understand if I had any reservations about investing so much time in her. She wasn't convinced that she was a "worthwhile project." I asked her if she was ready to invest time and energy. She was ready if I was ready.

This conversation stayed with me. It did not fit together with the impression of motivation that she otherwise conveyed. I was left with the feeling that I would have to talk her into finding life worthwhile, for she had communicated her inner state of emptiness after all.

Following this introduction, we worked on her conflicts with her children. Most of this revolved around her daughter, who took so much for granted, helped herself to whatever she could get her hands on, and failed to live up to her mother's idea of morality. We made several attempts to see connections between this situation and her own childhood. Throughout, the analysand's mother remained a strangely indefinite figure. She had given birth to seven children, two of whom she lost to polio at two and three years of age. She was a hard worker, but she always hummed a tune to herself. When I asked her to describe this in more detail, she told me that they weren't so much real songs as melancholy themes. She didn't recall any conflicts with her mother. She was convinced that it was not possible to have any conflicts; her mother always gave in.

She had not seen much of her father. He had been preoccupied with his business. As she grew older, he would talk to her about what was going on in the business. He praised her budding sense for business affairs. The second eldest child, she was her father's confidant. Her elder sister had established a stronger bond with her mother. After serving an apprenticeship, the analysand worked steadily in her father's business. After he retired, she took it over and restructured it. Her father had at first been skeptical about the changes she made, but then grew increasingly proud. She took over the business eight years before the analysis.

Now and then she brought in a dream which we worked over in depth. Our relationship was friendly, but I kept asking myself why she was in analysis and whether this was really the right thing for her. She treated me as if I were a mother with many "children" to take care of. She went out of her way not to be a burden. This made me feel inwardly aggressive. I told her that I felt so protected by her that it was starting to get on my nerves. Had she felt this way toward her mother? All such interpretations, which seemed correct to me and gave me a measure of relief after saying them, received her kind and patient consideration.

The first forty-four hours of therapy brought about a change in her feelings toward herself. It made her happy when she remembered dreams. We worked on each dream with the help of active imagination. I would invite her to enter back into the dream images and to let the feelings in these images take hold of her again. She began to take more time for her personal life. She became more aware of how she felt about different members of the family. She discovered more patience for her daughter. She felt that she was making progress in therapy.

After about a year of therapy, during which she came twice a week except during long breaks when she or I was gone, she brought into the forth-fifth hour a dream that shocked her.

> Dream: *I am in the town square. My hands are to be cut off. I am terrified. It really happens: someone cuts off my hands. It doesn't hurt as much as I expected, but now what should I do? I can't go on without hands.*

She reported that she had started from her sleep with a scream. After listening to the dream, her husband had assured her that it was possible to live without hands; she should go back to sleep. This response infuriated her. She told me that she even had the fantasy of cutting his hands off. This fantasy made things worse. She didn't know that she had such an aggression for him. But then again, neither did she feel any particular love. Their erotic life had seen better days, but otherwise, they were well suited to each other.

The morning after the dream she wanted to call me. But when she thought about how her husband had reacted to her anxiety, she was afraid that I would find it overblown as well. When she came to the session four days later, she told me the dream without emotion. But the dream alarmed me. Its emotional quality was totally different from any of her other dreams. She perceived the shock it caused me. She noticed my ripple of emotional insight: so this is the hidden problem in this person's life! "I suppose I could have called you after all," she confessed, describing how her husband had made her feel.

Then we entered into the images of her dream in the usual way. The town square reminded her of the church square in which she had grown up, as well as the square in her present neighborhood. The square in the dream was different in that it had no trees or other surroundings. This dream square made her feel uneasy—it was so barren and cold.

She was not sure who had cut off her hands or exactly where that had happened. But the image of being without hands was very clear, as was the blood. Despair: she would never be able to live without hands. For the first time, she broke down and cried. I asked her to allow as much space as possible for the feeling that came with the image of cut-off hands. Then she should see if she could put it into words.

"I have no more hands to give to anyone. I am becoming completely dependent on others. I feel so helpless. I can't reach out and take anything for myself. I cannot reach out to anyone else and touch them. Talking is the only way I know how to relate. My business is not the problem; the problem is I can't use my hands to comfort anyone. And I can't hit with them either. I don't come near anyone with my hands. If I did, they would cut them off."

I asked who "they" referred to.

Her husband, she replied, who told her she was being hysterical. Her brother: she had asked him if he would like to sell the part of the business that he was having trouble with. "Don't get your hands mixed up in my stuff!" he had told her only about a week before. This response had cut to the quick; she had only wanted to help. She realized he was jealous. After all, she had enjoyed much greater success than he. A memory occurred to her: once she wanted to help her mother take care of an infant. "Keep your dirty hands away," her mother snapped.

A stream of memories was unleashed, all having to do with not being able to "lend a hand" or take what she wanted from life. Once she wanted to go dancing. Her father shamed her: not simply forbidding, he told her that if she wanted to act like a primitive, there was nothing he could do about it. Naturally, she did not want to seem primitive to her father.

Suddenly she realized that she had turned her childhood feelings against her own daughter, whom she had prevented from ever being able to take anything for herself. At most, she had been allowed to take only that which spelled achievement. For the first time, she felt admiration for her daughter, who hadn't let her hands be cut off.

I, too, had "cut off the hands" of my analysand, in part by not allowing her to treat me with "kid gloves." I had rejected her gentle touch. It was no wonder she had not dared to reach out to me after the horrible dream. The theme was now constellated. Her recall of her past in terms of this symbol was more intensely lit up with emotion than ever before. We also understood the analytical relationship in terms of this image. Could therapy end up being a crippling experience, taking away her hands?

The complex of severed hands was constellated, especially in relation to her husband, but also to work colleagues. Her reactions to my limits or supposed limits were overblown, and the complex confused me with someone from work who had been cutting her off. It became increasingly difficult for me to get hold of anything at all in our work. I ended up keeping my hands off of everything. I spoke with her about these feelings of mine, hoping to thus come into contact with hers. Such moments of contact had been rare. She now discovered in what aspect of her life she most painfully felt the effects of the unknown person in her dream. Everyone seemed to band against her to keep her from using her hands to help herself, to stroke and comfort, to reach out assertively in relating to others. This memory work helped her to realize that while she had good, strong hands for business, she hadn't any for personal relationships.

In the fifty-first hour I asked her to imagine what she would like to do with her hands. I eased her into a guided fantasy by inviting her to touch and caress her own hands.

"I wish my hands could stroke and comfort. I think there are times when I could express my feelings so much better with my hands than with my tongue, if I could only caress. I want to walk together with someone, hand in hand. I want to feel warmth. I want to give warmth. That is only something I have been able to do with my children. I was always too embarrassed to do it with adults. But I wouldn't be anymore. Do you find it embarrassing?"

I assured her that I don't find it embarrassing. It makes for a feeling of trust.

She spoke at length about her longing to trust. If only she could just take a hug or a kiss for herself. She became poetic in describing a warm relationship in which she could get what she wanted.

She must learn to help herself in life, she resolved. She should be less influenced by what others think is right. Her daughter posed a challenge here: could she hold on to what she thought was right?

My intervention not only put the past in a new light. The imaginative exercise brought alive the dimension of anticipation that was also part of the symbol. Invited to consider what she would like to do with her hands, she began to long for a relationship that would make life more satisfying.

But her longing was miles from fulfillment. On center stage at the moment was a woman with her hands cut off. At once, this was a woman who was repeatedly stopped short of taking what she wanted yet one who could not help herself to what she wanted. She could not arrange her personal life the way she wanted. Slowly, the quality of her desperation began to change: it became less of an outward grasping and more of an inward grappling.

"Am I the only one with this problem?" she once asked. In response, I told her the fairy tale called "The Girl Without Hands." I told her the version that is still part of the German folktale tradition (see the end of this article for entire tale).

The fairy tale is found in many parts of the world. Generally, it consists of the following narrative elements:

1. The heroine's hands are severed. The reasons in different versions of the tale are: she will not marry her father; her father has sold her to the devil; she gives alms against her father's expressed will; her sister-in-law is jealous and slanders her; her stepmother (or mother) is jealous.
2. The heroine leaves the place of her misery and comes to the court of a king. The king marries her.
3. She becomes pregnant, and the king is called to war just as she is about to give birth. She is banished a second time after someone mixes up letters or gives false information. Depending on the version, this may be her in-laws, her father, her mother, her sister-in-law, or the devil.

4. After a long period of hardship and wandering in the forest, a miracle causes her hands to grow back—as a rule, in connection with her care and concern for her children.
5. The king returns from war and searches for his wife and children. He finds them.

The fairy tale suggests that various situations in life can lead to a feeling that women's hands have been cut off and that they have to go on without them. As if victims of some horrible tragedy, they make their way in the world without hope. They resign themselves to being crippled. Yet these women always find their way to a place where they can nourish themselves. There they meet a king and join up with him.

But matters are not so easily resolved. The old problem returns. The complexes rear up their heads again. New possibilities now exist (newborn children), but the hands have not yet grown back. A development has taken place, but the problem can only be resolved once the hands are restored.

It is not only through devotion to the children, but also by taking control of her own life that the heroine's hands grow back. Resolve to never let the children be taken away again gives her the power to trust in life. The hands grow back through the certainty that nothing can come between her and her children.

Strangely enough, this fairy tale suggests that the problem of severed hands prevents an easy alliance with the man. The heroine has to leave the king again and endure a time of loneliness lasting seven years. The tale suggests that the very thing that holds us together must also be sacrificed. Perhaps this sacrifice is necessary because her original hold on men—in most tales the father or brother—had been all too strong.

I guided my analysand into a state of deep relaxation which allowed her a vivid experience of the images of the tale. At first, she was very surprised to discover that the image of her dream corresponded to a common motif in fairy tales. "But the fairy tale has a solution," she noted with joy. "And what a crazy one: she only has to stop believing that she cannot take things into her own hands."

The first thing that struck her about the tale was the father's failure to pay more attention to his daughter's feelings. She had cried but he didn't ask her for an explanation. He completely missed the danger she was in. The analysand's emotional reaction to this first consisted of regret, followed by anger, and various memories arose.

Then she became preoccupied with a scene in which the mother is dying of thirst. When one of her children nearly slips into the water, she forgets that she does not have any hands. The analysand played and replayed this scene in her imagination. At first she thought that she was just playing it back like a recording. Although she found this uncreative and emotionally dishonest, the images would not leave her. Sometimes they would even flash in her mind during business meetings, to her great joy and surprise.

Suddenly she understood why the girl without hands could not stay at the king's court: she could not assume responsibility both for herself and for his children. The court was really his, not hers. The fact that he had left it in her hands meant that he was not any more capable of taking his life into his hands than she. It was somehow more natural to him to war with his hands than to care.

She applied these thoughts to her concrete situation. She kept having the feeling that someone was cutting her hands off. But gradually the certainty was growing in her heart that we can come to our own aid when we are in danger of losing something that we are sure belongs to us. Slowly, it was dawning on her what her children really meant to her at this time in her life. Through her imaginative journeys, she realized that they corresponded to her newly discovered affection for people, animals, and life in general. Slowly, she lost the sense of having her hands cut off. She began to feel that her hands were tied, but only in specific moments.

Since we had begun working with the fairy tale, a noticeable change had taken place in the therapeutic relationship as well. For one thing, she stopped accusing me of cutting off her hands. Most importantly, the fairy tale gave us a new focus. Both of us turned our attention to the tale. I was accompanying her in her imagination, entering into her images and feelings, but at the same time, I was developing my own images and feelings that had some degree of influence on those of the analysand without my expressing them. And she learned to make better use of me. She would ask me to tell her a certain part of the tale again. Or she would describe how she saw a certain passage and then ask me if I saw it that way, too. She became much less dependent on my judgment—or at least on what she assumed to be my judgment. She became clearer, more assertive, and also more affectionate in therapy, and she found these changes easy to translate into her life. Her feelings of emptiness loosened their hold of her. The analysis continued out of her own self-curiosity.

Working with fairy tales and myths allows us to make use of the images and image-spawning processes that reside as the motifs in the human imagination. But we can only do so when a comparable symbol has been activated in our own psyche and when we enter the fairy tale at an emotional level. These images stimulate our own fantasy, laying us open to the infectious power of hope that is expressed in so many tales. Fairy tales have the power to convince analysands that even their problems are not irresolvable, no matter how singular they may seem. In a way, myths and fairy tales can function like transitional objects. The personal mother is replaced by a collective ground of human mothering. It is like a deep coffer full of images that we can take out and consider this way and that, finding in them suggestions for how to cope with the problems that confront us along our various ways through the world. Only rarely do we copy the solution offered by the image. Myths spark imaginative processes that are unique to each individual, alter deeply entrenched feelings, and accompany us in the practical business of restructuring our daily lives.

Conclusion

For me, the concept of an interactive field includes more than the experience of a "convergence" of the collective and personal unconscious. The interactive field can also help us locate processes that contribute to more conscious relationships. From a broad perspective, this means two persons engaging in a process of interpreting the factors that influence them both consciously and unconsciously. Factors of influence such as complexes need to be admitted to consciousness and become familiar parts of our experiential worlds. The less conscious and familiar they are (to the point of being completely unconscious), the more we fend them off, and the more we feel disoriented. Symbolic forms such as fairy tales broaden the interactive field between analalyst and analysand without breaking all boundaries. Symbols allow the closeness of deep understanding without crowding. Lack of distance provokes destructive maneuvers of defense.

Imaginative work allows a sharing of the interactive field without depriving analysands of their own point of view. This gives them the greatest possible chance of following a developmental course toward which the psyche itself is heading.

Later interpretations of this imaginative experience need not reduce the autonomy of the psyche. If they take account of the process of interaction as well as the meaning of a symbol for the analysand's situation in life, interpretations are not demonstrations of greater knowledge but rather legitimate and necessary steps toward orientation.

The Girl Without Hands

Once there was a widower who had a daughter who often visited the woman living next door. She would have her hair combed in return for which she would help out with whatever chores there were. The woman had also been widowed. One day the girl pleaded with her father to marry the widow. After a long period of indecision, he decided to do it, and the widow agreed.

The widow brought her own daughter to the marriage as well, and when both girls had grown up and were of marrying age, there were plenty of interested young men coming to call. But the daughter of the man was more beautiful than the daughter of the woman. She was preferred by the young men who came to call, and this did not go over well with the woman at all. She became so sick with jealousy that one day she decided to do her stepdaughter in. The girl brought food to her father in the forest every day, so the old woman made a deal with some thieves who agreed to catch her and kill her there.

One day the thieves stopped the girl on her way through the forest.

"Where are you going?"

"I am bringing my father's midday meal."

"Go ahead, but be sure to come back the way you came."

The girl was so frightened that she began to cry.

"What are you crying about?" asked her father. But she didn't dare say a word and went right back the way she had come.

The thieves stopped her and argued among themselves about what they should do with her. She cried so hard that they couldn't bring themselves to kill her. But they had to bring the old woman some proof of their deed. "We'll poke out her eyes," one said. "We'll rip out her tongue," said another. The third said, "We'll hack off her hands." And that's what they did: they cut off her hands and let her go.

The girl wandered for a long, long time and got very tired and hungry. Finally, she came to an orchard with all kinds of fruit trees, but since she had no hands with which to pick, she bit into the apples and pears hanging on the tree.

The orchard belonged to a king. One day, he was taking a walk there when he happened to notice that the fruit on the lower branches had been bitten into. He wondered what sort of animal would do that. He went for another walk in the evening, and the girl was there, too. When the wind blew and bent a branch toward her, she bit into a pear. The king spoke up and asked her how she had gotten into the orchard.

Although she was very frightened, she told the king what had happened to her in the forest, how the thieves had cut off her hands, how she had found nothing to eat until she had stumbled onto the fruit trees. The king was immediately entranced by her beauty, and felt sorry for her, too. He took her back to his castle, and they were married soon after.

It wasn't long before the king was called to war, and while he was away, the woman gave birth to twins. The old queen couldn't stand the sight of them and wrote a letter to the king in the battlefield saying that his woman had given birth to a dog and a cat. The king believed what he read in the letter and wrote back:"Do away with the girl." So they bound the young queen's two children to her breast and drove her off.

She wandered the entire day until she felt she would die of hunger and thirst. Finally she came to a fountain, but just as she was about to put her lips to the water, she noticed a sign that said,"Whoever drinks from this water will turn into a deer." So she resisted her thirst and went on further until she found another fountain. As she leaned over to drink, one of her children slipped out and nearly fell into the water. When she reached into the water to save her child with her handless arm, she felt her hand growing back under water. So she dipped her other hand into the water, and it grew back, too.

The poor woman was quite relieved. She wandered on, and when it got dark, she climbed up into a tree to see if she could spot a light. Far in the distance she saw a light and walked in that direction until she came to a house. The door was open. Inside, there was table set with food and drink. Since she and her children were very hungry, they sat right down and ate, and then lay down to sleep. There was a cow at the house and some chickens. They lived there for seven years, without a soul ever coming by.

Meanwhile, the king deeply regretted having ordered his wife to be driven away. After seven years had passed, he dreamed that he found her while on a hunt. So he summoned his helper and set forth on horseback into the forest. He came to the house where the woman was staying with her children and asked her for lodging. She recognized him immediately, but he didn't recognize her because she had hands. They ate supper together, and then the guests lay down to sleep. But the woman and the children set to work plucking feathers.

The king's helper didn't fall asleep. He kept watch and listened to what the woman said to the children. When the king, in his sleep, let one of his arms droop down over the side of the bed, the woman said to one of the children, "Go over there and lift your father's arm back up into bed." The little boy couldn't manage to lift the arm all by himself, so the second son went over and helped him. But then the king's foot slipped out and hung over the side of the bed. Again the mother said, "Go over there and lift your father's foot back into bed." And again it took both boys. After a while, the king's head was hanging over the side. The woman sent her sons but they couldn't lift it by themselves. So their mother went over herself, kissed the king's forehead, and lifted his head back into bed.

The next morning, the king and his helper returned to their hunt. While they were underway, the helper told the king what he had heard in the night. That evening, they returned to the same little house and asked for lodging again. The woman received them kindly and cooked them a fine dinner.

After dinner, the king lay down in bed but only pretended to sleep and let his hand hang down. So he heard for himself when the woman said,"Go over there and lift your father's arm back into bed." And since one boy couldn't lift it by himself, the other helped him. Then the king let his foot hang down again, and again the woman sent her sons. Finally, the king let his head hang over, and the woman came herself, kissed him, and lifted his head back into bed.

At last, the king opened his eyes and asked how she had known who he was. Was she really his wife? When she showed him the scars on her arms, the king sent his helper to fetch the royal coach. He drove home with his wife and sons and they lived happily ever after.

References

Heidegger, M. 1978. *Die Frage nach der Technik*. Vorträge und Aufsätze. 4. Auflage. Pfullingen: Neske.

Jung, C. G. 1921. *Psychological Types.* In *CW*, vol. 6. Princeton, N.J.: Princeton University Press, 1971.

Kast, V. 1990. *Die Dynamik der Symbole*: *Grundlagen der Jungschen Psychotherapie.* Olten: Walter.

Whitcher, D., trans. *Deutsche Volksmärchen.* 1966. Köln: Diederichs, pp. 231–234.

Wiesenhütter, E. 1969. *Therapie der Person.* Stuttgart: Hippokrates.

Willi, J. 1975. *Die Zweierbeziehung.* Reinbek bei Hamburg: Rowohl.

Response to Verena Kast's
"A Concept of Participation"

Luigi Zoja

Since the importance of analysts' own emotions became known and they were encouraged to undergo training analysis themselves, no one has believed that analysis is centered on the understanding of just one person, the patient.

But listening casually to the talk given by Verena Kast and by others at this conference, one might arrive at the equally simplistic conclusion that analysis involves just two people: the analyst and the patient. Perhaps even the title of this conference—Interpretation and the Interactive Field—contributes to this oversimplification, not because it is wrong, in and of itself, but because, if we take it too literally, we think of a field occupied by just two people.

Things are not that simple. I believe that this field we talk about is trod by an infinite number of people, both from one's individual and from one's collective past. The past and society cannot be excluded from it.

Luigi Zoja is a Jungian analyst in Milan, Italy. He is a teacher and training analyst at the C. G. Jung Institute of Zurich and a training analyst at the Centro Italiano di Psicologia Analitica. He is the author of *Drugs, Addiction, and Initiation: The Modern Search for Ritual* and *Growth and Guilt: Psychology and the Limits of Development.*

This point of view does not clash with Kast's, but it expands on one aspect implicit in her idea of participation and, more generally, in the work of any Jungian. As we saw in the diagram depicting transference and countertransference, the adjective *collective* is substituted for the adjective *personal* at the deepest levels of the analyst-patient relationship.

The mystery status, which Kast ably described as a phase of analysis, is not a phenomenon unique to psychotherapy or to the personal lives of the participants involved in the analytic process. Mystery, and the related concept of mysticism (derived from the same root word) characterize not only individual experience but also entire segments of Western history.

Kast has indicated (pp. 42-43) how the mystery status—the renunciation of the demand to know, and the fusion of the deepest psychic layers—unites patient and analyst.

Generally speaking, mystery is not a negative—a lack of knowledge or awareness—but a state in which fusion is experienced as solemn participation, which is of opposite and much greater value than distinction. In fact, differentiation and distinction may actually feed knowledge, while mystery participation makes one feel at one with life, with the cosmos, with God.

If we were to translate this into psychological terms, we would say that distinction implies ego values and fusion implies the unconscious (and, at certain times, the self).

What concerns us here is that a pressing need for mystery fusion, so great that it burns like wildfire, proliferates during certain periods of our cultural history. (Like firefighters, the ego and the superego are unable to put out such flames).

During the period of the *dolce stil novo*, for example, which appeared in Italy toward the end of the Middle Ages, great feelings of fusion were constellated in the relationships between men and women. The fusion experience is so strongly spiritual that we can register it as an extension, at the human level, of the intimate union with God that characterized the great mystic experiences of the Middle Ages. The beloved seems to have been unattainable and unknowable, and yet the elusiveness didn't matter because it was as if the beloved had always been a part of the poet.

Another wave of passionate mystery originated in central Europe and spread into the whole Western culture in the nineteenth century. It was called Romanticism, and with it came extreme expressions of love, of feeling, of intimate belongingness to nature, and the rediscovery of one's own roots outside of civilization. To get a sense of the contact this epoch had with the previous wave, despite the centuries that separated them, one need think only of the intimacy with nature that characterized the thinking and religious poetry of St. Francis of Assisi.

What does all this have to do with analysis?

If it is true—as Neumann has asserted and we can back up at least to a certain degree—that the development of the psyche of an individual follows closely that of civilization (that is, ontogeny echoes phylogeny), then the need for mystery during certain periods of a person's life is profoundly related to society's need for mystery during certain historical periods; that is, they are expressions of the same archetypal drive.

But if it is also true—and it most certainly is—that the psyche is a self-regulating system and that different historical epochs activate different archetypes, then mystery status is not just a necessary regression for people whose lives lacked the fusional mystery experience (the "we" experience, according to Kast). It is also, perhaps, the necessary correction of unidirectional cultural movements.

The two epochs used as examples of fusional collective drives confirm this idea. The *dolce stil novo* flourished in Italy at a time when people were leaving the countryside for the city, leaving prayer for business and worldliness, and leaving the trustful contemplation of God for invention, travel, art, and knowledge. The navigator who once trusted God and His celestial representations, the stars, now turned to a product of human technology, the compass, for guidance.

(Please note the possible analogies of this historical course to our analytical work, in which an effort at distinction based on the will of the ego and on technique is superseded by a mystery status made up of transference and countertransference.)

Similarly, Romanticism supersedes to correct, if you will, the one-sided values of the age of Enlightenment: that is, the drive to discover, to progress, to develop. Against the supremacy of light, which lent its name to the period, Romanticism counters with evocations of the darkness of night and of forests. Instead of civilization, it celebrates animals, nature, and primitive peoples (those who, not by chance, have not forgotten *participation mystique*). It values instinct over reason. Put in psychological terms, Romanticism tries to correct the one-sided values of the ego by reemphasizing the unconscious.

I want to stress that these feelings of collective fusional mystery are not different from individual ones, but are part of one archetypal pattern of experience, widespread during certain historical epochs (out of a need to correct a one-sidedness) and awakened during analysis on an individual basis. Kast has reminded us that the idea of mystery status, applicable to analysis today, actually dates back to romantic thought, by way of Novalis. But the most passionate and fusional forms of love are not to be found everywhere or always. Rather, they develop as a specific way of feeling at a certain historical moment, as in Europe as it approached modernity (Denis de Rougemont 1939, theory of *amour passion*).

From our point of view, this giving oneself up to fuse with another cannot be taken only in its literary and cultural form, but also as self-therapy for all of society, as an attempt to self-regulate the collective psyche.

Seen this way, it no longer seems merely coincidental that analysis was born toward the end of the Romantic era, coming from those countries and articulated in that language—German—which had characterized the origin of Romanticism.

The more fusional transference—that is, a less technical and more archetypal state uniting the patient and analyst in a "mystery status"—was an embarrassing, irrational, and uninvited guest for the initiators of psychoanalysis. But from our point of view, fusional transference is an unconscious expression of the inevitable need for correction, a specific message in the general struggle between Western enlightenment and romanticism.

This difference of opinion is evident also in the contrast between Freud and Jung: Freud called transference "neurosis" and tried to employ techniques to resolve it, while Jung, inspired by a more romantic vision, evoked archetypal kinship and hope of a religious nature in his dealings with patients: "So, if a patient projects the saviour complex into you, for instance, you have to give back to him nothing less than a saviour" (1935).

Unfortunately, despite the cyclical recurrence of specific archetypal needs, and despite the cultural corrections such as that of the Romantic movement, the collective in which we live continues to move in an egoic direction—toward rationality and scientific distinction, thereby feeding what Jung called the hubris of consciousness. Fusional mystery, therefore, cannot but lose ground in the collective conscience.

For example, breastfeeding is a fusional sort of experience that has been reappraised of late, but not because of a general return of fusional states. Just the opposite: the reappraisal is born of a better technical understanding of early infancy. In sum, in a society that is increasingly nonideological, less transcendental, and more materialistic, a mystic fusion with God is as unimaginable as a love affair with an extraterrestrial. Mystic unity has been replaced in the minds of the majority by the "mystique of things" (Baudrilland 1970). Unfortunately, these "things" are solid, so one can never hope truly to fuse and become one with them.

Has what I've said been too general to be applicable to our analytic work? Jung reminds us that psychic suffering is never only personal, but has its roots in the neuroses of the entire culture. Naturally, I agree with Kast on the decisive importance that a profound participation capable of suspending even the need for consciousness—that is, a mystery status—can have in reactivating a self-regulatory dynamic in a patient's psyche. I would like to add only that, generally speaking, this healing experience may become increasingly important, since experiences of the indistinct "we" in our nonideological society are becoming briefer, more self-centered, and more limited to earliest infancy. Theoretically, to go back to my example, it could help if mothers of newborns were taught the importance of fusional mystery, but this is extremely difficult to do because fusional mystery is increasingly and implicitly taboo, in the sense that it is the antithesis of knowledge and efficiency. (It is this sort of cultural taboo, rather than a strictly sexual taboo, which is responsible for much of the erotic dysfunction in present-day society. More than impotence and frigidity, the inability to reach orgasm is difficult to reconcile, because orgasm is the acceptance of fusional regression on a physiological level.)

It is therefore probable that the fusional mystery experience will be an increasingly frequent, albeit unconscious, request that patients will put to their analysts.

The "protected reserves" in which this "primitive" state can be truly experienced during infancy are dwindling; and if the state is not experienced until later, it is apt to be in a way that is rougher, consumption-oriented, and insensitive—in the form of fanatical sects, political groups motivated more by hysteria than by altruism, barbarians disguised as sports fans, and self-styled music enthusiasts who are really just drug enthusiasts.

I hope I have not lost anyone with my digressions and that I have been persuasive in arguing that not only two people are present in participation and in the mystery status, and that the confines of the interactive field extend much farther.

References

Baudrilland. 1970. *La societe de consommation*. Paris: Denoël.
de Rougemont, D. 1939. *L'amour et l'Occident:* Paris: Plon.
Jung, C. G. 1935. *The Tavistock Lectures*, *CW* 18, lecture V, par. 352. Princeton, N.J.: Princeton University Press.

The Field of Sleep

Murray Stein

> *Now see the god, his bough*
> *A-drip with Lethe's dew, and slumberous*
> *With Stygian power, giving it a shake*
> *Over the pilot's temples, to unfix,*
> *Although he fought it, both his swimming eyes.*
> *Aeneid*, Book V

The Case of William

There is an interactional field over which the god Somnus reigns. Occasionally one finds oneself in it in analysis. There the air is heavy with "Lethe's dew," and a "Stygian power" draws the eyelids forcefully downward. Like Palinurus, the unlucky helmsman of Aeneas's ship, who is the target of Somnus's interest and ends up dropping from his vessel into the water at the touch of the god's hypnotic bough, the analyst may fight valiantly but perhaps unsuccessfully to resist the compelling force of drowsiness.

Murray Stein, Ph.D., is the author of *In MidLife, Jung's Treatment of Christianity,* and *Solar Conscience/Lunar Conscience.* He is the editor of the Chiron Clinical Series and of *Jungian Analysis* (Open Court) and the author of numerous articles. He is a training analyst at the C. G. Jung Institute of Chicago and has a private practice in Wilmette, Illinois.

When William first entered my office, he looked like a big sleepy child. He stated his age as twenty-something, but my thought was that he must be, psychologically speaking, an overgrown seven-year-old. He was of average height and overweight to the point of having little definite shape. His round face revealed none of the contours of adulthood. With his hair closely cropped, he had the appearance of an angelic child of latency age.

He smiled readily, could appear thoughtful and reflective, but mostly he seemed to be "absent," gazing into the far distance and absorbed in his own inner world. His dress was casual, as fit the life of a student, and during the year that I saw him in analysis he wore only thin tennis shoes, even in the depths of a brutal Chicago winter.

From the beginning, it was a struggle for me to stay awake during sessions with William. It must be confessed that this can happen to me in individual sessions with almost anyone. (I have spoken to many other analysts about the problem of sleepiness in sessions, and all confirm having such a problem occasionally.) For me, sleepiness is generally a function of how well I slept the night before, or of the time of day it might be (after lunch and early afternoon are the most trying), or of the degree to which a patient is present emotionally or stimulating in a particular session or is blocked or resistant to the pain of analytical uncovering. But it is rarely the case that an individual is able to cast a strong hypnotic spell over me on a regular basis no matter what the time of day or what else of interest might be happening. William had the hypnotic force with him, and from the first session onward, I had to struggle to keep my eyes open and my hands on the helm of the analytic vessel.

Typically, William would enter the office with a floating, ambling sort of gait, take his place on the couch, gather himself together a bit, and proceed to stare off dreamily into empty space. As I sat across from him and observed his face, I would wait quietly and seek to enter the vacant silence with him. Eventually, he would begin to speak. It might be about his chronic struggle with food and overeating (he had always been overweight and at times in his life was obese) or his difficulties with schoolwork (self-discipline eluded him and deadlines always caught him unawares) or with schoolmates. He had come to me originally because of depression and a lack of motivation at school, and I expected this to occupy us for a while. But whatever the topic might be, the hypnotic aura was always present. An initial surge of energy that produced some verbalization would be followed by long silences during which William's eyes would glaze over, his face would assume an expression of soft vacancy, and several minutes would pass before another momentary burst of energy brought him back into the room with me.

Sometimes, I would respond to one of these verbalizations with a comment or a question or even with an attempt to interpret (there might be a link to something else from a previous session or to earlier history). Generally these produced an acknowledgment (he was not rude) or even a response that would elaborate the theme with further associations, but this energy soon ran its course, and we would return to silence.

There are many kinds of silence in analysis: the pregnant pause that brings a new thought or perspective; the angry silence that seeks to punish; the painful silence of conflict and mental paralysis; the desperate silence of despair. To me, William's silence felt like a void. There seemed to be no content to it. It was not, at first, unpleasant but simply empty and vacant and extremely hypnotic. I sometimes asked him where he had been during such a silence. Usually he could not tell me much about the content of his thoughts during that period, and he would drift back to his somnolent state. If I interrupted a silence, he would shake himself and gaze at me in surprise, as though I had just awakened him from sleep and was asking him to recount a dream. Again, he could not give a very satisfactory account of mental contents during the silence. This was blank mindlessness.

Upon the islands of consciousness that were gradually built up during the course of some fifty sessions, we did erect quite a bit of structured material—a detailed personal history, a sense of the psychodynamics in various important relationships, a fairly careful definition of several key conflicts—but the overall impression of this analytic encounter, in retrospect, is of vast stretches of empty sea divided up by several pieces of solid land and the presence of Somnus throughout the voyage. Over and over, it was as though

> Now dewy Night had touched her midway mark
> Or nearly, and the crews, relaxed in peace
> On their hard rowing benches, took their rest,
> When Somnus, gliding softly from the stars
> Put the night air aside, parted the darkness,
> Palinurus, in quest of you. (*Aeneid* V:839–844)

And I was the hapless Palinurus. But so was William.

For me, the struggle with Somnus began the moment William ambled into the office. Eventually it became so severe that his physical presence alone was a cue for me to want to nod off. I never did actually fall asleep completely, but many times my head touched the waters, and I would pull myself up from them with a start. The fantasy that came to me occasionally was of being mesmerized by a snake or by a snake charmer. The air would thicken, my eyes became heavy, my mind utterly blank, and only by the greatest effort of will was I able to hang on to the slightest shred of consciousness. It was not that William was boring (see Khan 1986 on the "boring patient"); the sessions were not painful in the way that boredom "bores" and irritates. William was hypnotic.

I wondered if he had this same effect on other people. The opportunity to find out came about when he moved to another city and began working with an analyst there to whom I had referred him. At a professional meeting, this analyst thanked me for the referral, and I asked him in a general way about how things were going with William. "Oh wonderfully! He's such an interesting case!" I could honestly agree, William's case was interesting, but I fished a little further to see if this analyst had also felt the mesmerizing force I had found so prominent. It seemed he had not! I was astounded, and this is still a puzzle to me. Was William completely different with him? Or was this other analyst so completely different from me that he was not affected by Somnus or did not constellate the Somnus factor with William? Perhaps Somnus was not interested in him. Or perhaps he was not telling me the whole truth about his experience of William for fear that I would think poorly of him; I, too, had not told him about William's mesmerizing effect on me. (Communicatons among analyst colleagues are usually heavily disguised, not only for reasons of confidentiality but also for reasons of self-esteem and persona preservation.)

The Interactional Field

The case of William has become for me one of the most graphic and convincing experiences of an "interactional field" in analysis. The idea of a field in analysis is borrowed from physics, where fields of force, such as a magnetic field, are described and analyzed. A field is a pattern of energy flow that affects objects in its domain. In a psychic field, psychodynamic forces are at work, usually at a mostly unconscious level, and these produce particular states of consciousness in both analyst and analysand. *Projection, projective identification, participation mystique, transference/ countertransference processes, fusion* are all terms used, in various contexts in the literature, to think about such interactive fields. We are at a point now in the development of analytic thought where we can use myth and image to name and define the kinds of fields that are constellated in analysis and thus obtain a more detailed map of analytic territory than we have had by being limited to one or another of these abstract terms.

One kind of field often mentioned in the literature of analytical psychology is the erotic field. Eros launched psychoanalysis and has been central for discussions of the analytic relationship for the past nine decades. Eros defines the classic interactive field. Ares, the god of aggression and conflict, defines another well known and much studied field. What I am proposing is that there are many other fields as well, each of which deserves scrutiny, discussion, investigation, and a name. The field of sleep, the realm of Somnus, is the one under consideration here.

This field, which might also be called a field of poppies, is soporific. In it, both analyst and analysand want to nod off or drop into a state of more or less complete unconsciousness.

There is a spectrum of conditions in this field. At one extreme, there is a pull toward sleep that is practically irresistible; at the other end, there is only a mild, barely even perceptible, gentle, lulling, numbing seduction, a slight drift in the direction of nodding off or passively daydreaming, a gradual slippage away from tracking what is going on. How strong the magnetic force of Somnus happens to be in a particular case will depend on the size and power of the complex that supports it.

Diagnosing the Field

To obtain a grip on the psychological nature of this field, diagnostic categories and developmental perspectives can be helpful. While the danger of freezing a human being in the icy box of a diagnosis is always a hazard and to be avoided, a diagnosis, along with a developmental understanding of the genesis of psychological structure, can guide us as we try to penetrate more deeply and empathically into subtle layers of the unconscious psyche surrounding the symptomatic surface and to discern possibilities for further analytic insight.

So how would William be diagnosed? Among the preoedipal possibilities (for he was clearly preoedipal and existed almost entirely in the world of the Mother), both of the two standard ones, narcissistic personality disorder and borderline personality disorder, fit to a degree. He did show some evidence of the "extreme self-absorption, lack of empathy, inability to accept criticism, and grandiose and exhibitionistic needs" of the narcissistic personality (Schwartz-Salant 1989, p. 55). Also there were features characteristic of impenetrable narcissistic defenses. Aspects of the borderline disorder were evident as well. He did demonstrate the typical kind of "environmental enmeshment" (ibid., p. 56) that borderlines show, although the rage and abuse that therapists so frequently experience with borderline patients were absent. Perhaps these would have come out if the analysis had continued longer.

William lived on the margin, socially speaking; often he felt himself to be an outsider and even an outcast, and he had a bone to pick with those who represented the establishment. He would quietly first idealize and then denigrate important persons in his surroundings, the way borderline personalities typically do, and yet he seemed more than borderline. In a sense, he was over the border, but he was not manifestly psychotic, and he did not routinely confuse fantasy and reality. His was a type of consciousness that goes into and out of autisticlike states which alternate with normal interpersonal awareness. These could be thought of as fugue states, but momentary ones and quite easily interrupted. To capture William diagnostically, I found Thomas Ogden's description of the autistic-contiguous position a good fit.

Ogden writes of a "mode of generating experience" that is "the most primitive," in which "psychic organization is derived in large part from sensory contiguity, that is, connections are established through the experiences of sensory surfaces 'touching' one another" (1989, p.31, n.6). The autistic-contiguous position is an extension of the Kleinian depressive and paranoid-schizoid positions into an earlier and, in adults, a more regressed and primitive type of mental organization. The autistic-contiguous mode of experience is characteristic of early infancy and is "built upon the rhythm of sensation (Tustin), particularly the sensations at the skin surface (Bick)" (ibid., p. 31). The ego's experience is nonreflective here, and the major features of experiencing are rhythm and surface contiguity with objects (ibid., p. 32). A regression to this mode of experiencing in analysis looks not only preverbal but presymbolic (there are no clear images or thoughts present), and while this state is not autistic in the strict definition of childhood pathology, it is profoundly diffuse.

Ogden lists a number of typical countertransference reactions to the patient who is in the autistic-contiguous position, among which is the following:

> At times, the space between the patient and myself has felt as if it were filled with a warm soothing substance. Frequently, this is associated with a dreamy countertransference state that has nothing to do with boredom. It is a rather pleasant feeling of being suspended between sleep and wakefulness. (Ibid., p. 44)

This is a reference to a state that Bion calls reverie, an ideal state of the nurturing mother when she is emotionally in intimate contact with her infant and laying the groundwork for "alpha function" in the infant's incipient mind.

There is, however, also a typical kind of anxiety associated with the autistic-contiguous position. According to Ogden, there is "an unspeakable terror of the dissolution of boundedness resulting in feelings of leaking, falling, or dissolving into endless, shapeless space" (ibid., p. 81). This terror can also be experienced in the countertransference. In my work with William, this was felt as a terror of falling into the clutches of Somnus, of drowning in sleepiness. This was not the pleasant feeling of reverie, but rather a fear of being drawn by a forceful undertow toward a dark void of empty blankness. In Bion's terminology, we were threatened by a pull into mental territory that contained no alpha function and could therefore be exposed to beta elements lurking in the hidden recesses of the unconscious. I sensed at times the dim shape of a sinister presence. Later I would learn that this was the shape of a psychotic mother, who presented a threat of death by suffocation.

Staying Awake in the Countertransference

How much can one learn from a single case? This is an open question. It is possible to overgeneralize, to leap from a single instance to assuming that this describes a whole class of clinical phenomena. But it is also true that the "field" which I experienced with William in such extreme and sustained form is one that I have registered momentarily and less intensively with many analysands. There is a strong probability, I believe, that the unconscious dynamic forces and complexes which were operative in this case are active in many other cases, perhaps more subtly, but identically for all that. I do believe there is a field of sleep in which Somnus reigns, just as there is a field of love in which Eros holds sway. Many analysts and students have confirmed this in private discussions.

One could perhaps conceptualize this type of induced paralysis of mental alertness as an analysand's ego defense which works by creating a state of dissociation within and a wall of somnolence without. It could be seen as a defensive function whose purpose is to ward off the unwanted and intolerable intrusions of a disturbed mother. And the narcotic field may also function as a defense against psychic pain within: it is better to go to sleep than to feel despair, unconnectedness, and depression. For such a person to enter analysis and then proceed to fall asleep, dragging the analyst along into the poppy field, is like going to the dentist's office because one is suffering from a toothache but then refusing to open one's mouth because of the knowledge that drilling will hurt. But the tooth, rotten and decayed, hurts, too, and this was certainly part of William's dilemma.

This assessment of sleepiness as a defense seems accurate as far as it goes, but it does not tell the whole story, or even the most essential parts of the story. I do not completely subscribe to the notion that the field of sleep is only an ego defense, because I sense a much darker purpose behind the threat of Somnus. A defense—like denial, for instance—pretends to protect and sustain the individual's life, to have an adaptive function. But Somnus does not come on the scene with such benign intent. He wants Palinurus to drown; he wants death. There is a sinister design here that cannot be completely written off to defense.

The major effect of this hypnotic force is to produce a stagnant surface of consciousness, where, as in fairy tales of bewitchment, everyone is asleep. This spell is cast not to protect the sleepers but to halt life, growth, development. All movement toward individuation is stopped dead in its tracks. And anyone else who wanders into this field goes to sleep there, too.

Meanwhile, far beneath the surface of consciousness, there exists an intense but vague fantasy realm that is alive with activity. The only way to enter this territory is to pass the morphic test, to avoid the final effects of the drowsiness induced by (what I believe to be) the dark side of the mother complex. This seemed clearly to be the case with William. In his psyche, the mother complex generated a field of paralyzing bewitchment in which William's ego was trapped, and the main purpose of this was not to protect William but to hold him.

There are many fairy tales in which bewitchment takes the form of sleepiness and in this manner halts further development. Sleep freezes growth. "Snow White" and "Sleeping Beauty" are famous examples. "The Shoes That Were Danced to Pieces" (the Brothers Grimm) is a less well known tale in which the theme of being put to sleep plays a key role, and for my purposes here, it identifies the key elements needed by the analyst in order to survive and penetrate a psyche like William's. The story runs like this.

A king had twelve daughters whose shoes, each morning, were found worn out with dancing, despite his locking the door to their rooms and posting guards. The proclamation went out that whoever could discover how this happened could marry the princess of his choice. Death was the reward for failure. It happened that many princes accepted the challenge, but all failed because they fell asleep at the post. No one, it seemed, could stay awake through the night. While this powerful field of sleep held sway, the mystery continued and the princesses remained unwed.

The hero of the story receives some advice from an old woman who knows how the status quo is maintained. She tells him not to drink the wine the princesses will offer, and then to dress in the invisible cloak she will give him and follow the princesses wherever they go. In this way, he will discover their secrets. He does as he has been advised, and what he discovers is the secret life of the princesses. After dark, they go down into the earth through a trapdoor and walk through a magical garden. Each is rowed across a great lake by a corresponding prince and spends the night dancing wildly in a beautiful palace. At dawn they return, close the trapdoor, and act as if they had been sleeping all night. The hero is able to accompany them, silently and invisibly, and the next day he reports to the king what he has found. This breaks the spell. He marries the eldest daughter and inherits the kingdom. The princes, on the other hand, "were bewitched for as many days as they had danced nights with the twelve."

At the beginnings of analytic sessions with William, I often felt like the would-be hero of this fairy tale. The sessions began with a period of blank silence, and I would immediately feel the threat of Somnus in the atmosphere. I might make a comment, ask a question, refer to our last session—or not. Whatever I did or he did, the first minutes were spent by me trying to get used to the space. Gradually I acquired the ability to stay alert and to wait quietly (invisibly) until an opening appeared. William would seem to drop down into himself, and from there he might speak and reveal something of his inner life. Through many dark passages in the months we spent together, I was able to glimpse his childhood history with a psychotic mother, to witness the psychological incest that occurred between them, to understand the damage that was done to his sister (who was, by his account, intermittently psychotic and severely obese), and to acknowledge the valiant efforts he had made in vain to separate psychologically from his mother.

He also led me into the territory of his sexual fantasies and occasional activities. This was terrain that he protected to a great extent from everyone else. It was a secret and dangerous part of his life. Even his own ego would remain more or less asleep when he went there. This is where the princesses would dance the night away while his ego and his parental complexes slept. Here, his secret life ran on while all was quiet and asleep on the surface. In the morning, he would rise exhausted and not know quite why.

It took considerable time and patient effort to establish any clarity about what took place in this hidden fantasy territory, so vague at first were the stories and images that appeared. The scene, as it emerged into view, appeared to me childlike, paradisal, innocent. While sexuality was a prominent feature, it was not yet genital for the most part. There were scenes with boys and young men holding hands or dancing, being tender and intimate with one another, caring for each other. Nothing obscene or raw entered these pictures. They revealed great intensity and longing, feelings of deep communion in the gestures of holding and fondling. In these scenarios, vast amounts of time could be spent talking quietly and intently. There might be a momentary burst of Dionysian frenzy in the fantasies, but mostly they resembled a long, slow summer's day or a late evening at a club.

In the course of the year during which this brief analysis took place, William gained considerable capacity to put into words what was going on at this inarticulate level of fantasy activity. Some of the material was made up of memories, some of current wishes. There was at least one Great Mother fantasy in which William was being fed by a goddess directly through a tube.

As all of this material, especially the sexual images, became more integrated into his ego complex, and as William could accept having his liminal wishes and thoughts brought into consciousness with less conflict and fear, the fantasy scenes also gained in precision and lost some of their dark vagueness. At this point, we were less subterranean in our psychic explorations. Our sessions were also somewhat less soporific, although this element never vanished altogether.

In the single most important dream of the analysis, William finds himself trapped on his grandmother's farm. He comes upon his father's truck, however, and steals it to make an escape. He is on the way out, having overcome the greatest barriers, when he awakens. This dream preceded a good deal of ego consolidation and conscious strides toward individuation; it marked the initiation of a new stage in his development. We both immediately recognized the importance of this dream and referred to it often during the remainder of the analysis. It was the equivalent of the hero in the fairy tale winning a bride from among the twelve princesses who nightly danced their shoes to pieces. The emergence from the unconscious brought with it new energy and a stronger commitment to life and to real relationships.

Two Kinds of Sleep

What happened in the course of this analysis can be further amplified by another story about being put to sleep. According to the Yahwistic writer, God created first Adam and then the animals and birds to be his helpers. After Adam is asked to name the animals, God realizes that none is an adequate helper,

> So the Lord God caused a deep sleep to fall upon the man, and he slept, then he took one of his ribs and closed up its place with flesh. And the rib that the Lord God had taken from the man he made into a woman and brought her to the man. Then the man said, "This at last is bone of my bones and flesh of my flesh; this one shall be called Woman, for out of Man this one was taken." Therefore a man leaves his father and his mother and clings to his wife, and they become one flesh. (Gen. 2:21-24)

There is considerable and surprising isomorphism between this story from the Bible and the Grimms' fairy tale "The Shoes That Were Danced to Pieces," and also between these two tales and the case of William. The deepest points of contact have to do with two themes: the theme of separation from an identification with childhood images and figures, and the theme of creating a single anima figure with whom the ego complex (Adam in the Bible, the hero in the fairy tale, and William in my case) can relate.

In the biblical story, these themes are vividly presented. This passage from Genesis is often recited at weddings, which is an initiation ceremony with a rite of exit (giving the bride away), rites of liminality (the vows), and a rite of reincorporation (the return to society as a new couple). The note of leave-taking from the parental figures is unmistakable. This is clearly paralleled in the fairy tale, which also ends with a wedding and a child's consequent separation from the parental home.

Similar to the fairy tale, too, there is in the biblical story a movement from the "many" (i.e., the twelve princesses; all the animals and birds as helpers) to the "one" (i.e., the eldest princess only as bride; one woman, Eve). In both cases this represents a consolidation of the anima into a single psychic entity.

In the case of William, there was a gradual emergence (separation/individuation) from identification with the complexes of childhood (imaged dramatically in the dream of escape from his grandmother's farm in his father's truck) to a more conscious recognition of self/other distinctions and the beginnings, at least, of an integration of sexuality in his consciousness. He was gradually making his way out of the autistic-contiguous position.

Both fairy tale and biblical story end at the moment when explicit sexuality is constellated and imminent, and William's case also concluded at a point where his sexuality was being accepted consciously. The consolidation of the anima heralds the end of the smothering mother phase and the beginning of the dynamic anima phase of inner development. In a sense, the ego is born here for a second time, this time out of the psychological (as opposed to the physical) mother.

One crucial point of difference between the fairy tale and the biblical story, however, is the function of sleep in each. In the fairy tale, falling asleep while watching the princesses is a lethal failure and wakefulness is rewarded with the grand prize. Sleep supports the continuance of the pathological status quo. In the biblical story, on the contrary, sleep is the necessary condition for beginning individuation; it is a creative womb out of which the anima/mate is born. There are obviously different kinds of sleep or different functions and meanings to be assigned to the experience of falling asleep. Here, one is defensive and prevents individuation, the other is creative and facilitates individuation.

In William's life, both kinds of sleep were evident: the one was the narcotic field that was constellated in our sessions, a defensive screen thrown up by the mother complex to stifle development, to prevent separation, and to block fantasies from being registered by the ego; the other was the sleep of dreaming, which gave birth to the invaluable dream of stealing the father's truck and escaping from the grandmother's farm, a psychic event that was of great use to us in the analytic effort to free him from his mother-bound condition.

Perhaps this difference between two kinds of sleep rests on the fact that one is induced by a Father God who apparently wants the ego complex to solidify, unify, and individuate, at least to a certain degree, while the other is induced by an amorphous (in the fairy tale, no mother is mentioned) and (in William's case) highly disturbed mother complex. With William, it was important that analysis valued nocturnal dreams and used them to further individuation.

The Analyst's Interpretive Function in the Field of Sleep

"The Shoes That Were Danced to Pieces" indicates some hazards in trying to make analytic interpretations in this "field of sleep." The wise old woman who meets the hero on his way into town gives him two things: a piece of advice and an object. The advice is: "You must not drink the wine which will be brought to you at night, and you must pretend to be sound asleep" (p. 597). The object is a little cloak: "If you wear this, you will be invisible, and then you can steal after the twelve" (ibid.). By following these instructions, the hero is able to achieve his goal. This would suggest a prohibition on making sounds (i.e., giving conscious interpretations) in a case like this. An interpretation that prematurely ventures into the meaning of what is going on in this interactive field would disrupt the process.

Interventions from the side of consciousness, based as they usually are on theory and clinical experience, are dangerous. In fact, interpretations based on even the most specific material from a single case can have a disruptive effect when the field is constituted by strong features of an autistic-contiguous position. The premature presentation of edges, boundaries, conceptual formulations, subject-object differentiations, such as might be made in transference interpretations, have a startling effect and break the spell. The hero must go with the princesses into the underground caverns and simply observe what is there before reporting it to any part of the personality in treatment.

At one point in the story, the hero breaks a twig from a tree to take back with him as a token of where he has been. The tree "cracked with a loud report. The youngest cried out again: 'Something is wrong.'" (p. 598). This field is easily disturbed, like the surface of a quiet pond in the forest. The challenge is to stay alert in it, to observe what is going on, to bring back a report to the ego complex (the befuddled king, in our story) later, but at the moment of observation it is necessary to remain quiet and invisible.

In William's case, I, of course, made many "sounds." I observed, labeled, interpreted, educated, and even gave advice from time to time, but these sounds usually did not take place while we were in the narcotic field. Often at some point during the hour, or at the end of it, there would be a brief time to offer some clarifications and to hold ego-to-ego discussion and make some observations. At no time did I comment directly on the nature of the field itself. I did this out of instinct rather than theory or foresight. It seemed correct to go as far into the dissociated state with William as I could and to fetch back from it the bits of fantasy that gradually could be pieced together into what would eventually become a fairly clear image of his fantasies and desires, as well as his recollections from childhood.

On the Nature and Origin of Interactive Fields

Analytical cases eventually settle down into a particular pattern or image of interaction between the two persons involved in it. This image pattern, which characterizes the relationship and defines its deepest essence, lies at the heart of the interactive field. In another paper (1991), I wrote about "the muddle" being the core image of an interactive field in a particular analysis; it was a pattern of confusion and misunderstanding that endured throughout a rather lengthy analytic relationship. The pattern I am describing here, which typified my much shorter working relationship with William, was chiefly characterized by a kind of hypnotic stupor, by a strong pull toward deep unconsciousness.

How do these fields come into being? They may take form almost instantly, as was the case with William, or they may take a longer period of time to show their face. They are the product of the psychic alchemy that transpires in analysis, as described by Jung in "The Psychology of the Transference." These fields seem to constellate as a result of a particular mixture of specific psychic ingredients that are placed into the analytic container by both analysand and analyst.

Typically the analyst begins an analysis by quietly observing and taking in the spoken and unspoken communications of the new analysand (see Dieckmann 1991, chapter 2, for an excellent discussion of the initial session). This receptivity on the analyst's part in the initial session and several subsequent sessions allows a kind of psychic infection to take place in the analyst (Stein 1984). It is as though a psychic virus enters the field and finds a host body in the form of the analyst whom it can probe for entry. The virus fixes onto a psychic complex of the analyst's and probes for entry into it. Once it slips in, it begins to do its work of self-replication.

This penetration into the analyst's psyche by contents that are projected from the analysand's psyche (through "projective identification"—see Grotstein 1981) produces a state of psychic awareness in the analyst that is akin to that in the unconscious of the analysand. Generally it is dark, opaque, and confused at first. Jung spoke of this as "influence" and "psychic infection," and he referred frequently to the shamanic model of healing to discuss the analytic process. This transfer of psychic contents makes possible the almost miraculous "mind-reading" that analysts can often perform to the amazement of their analysands.

According to the shamanic model, the "illness" that the analysand suffers from is transferred to the analyst (a quite literal form of transference), and the analyst begins suffering from the same problem. Within the psyche of the analyst, there occurs a quasi-identification with the projection (a form of countertransference that is due to the response to the projection, called by Fordham syntonic countertransference), whereby the analyst makes the alien illness his or her own. Now the analyst not only can empathize in a highly precise way with the analysand but also can actually observe the analysand's psychic unconscious process at first hand, both for its destructive aspects and for the healing, restorative efforts that the presence of the virus constellates within the wider range of the psyche. One hopes that the analyst's psychic constitution is healthy and strong enough to withstand the illness and to counteract it with sufficient force to produce an antidote, although this is not always the case.

Some analysts succumb to the stronger personality and the virulent toxins of certain analysands and are badly injured or destroyed by them (for an excellent example of this, see Chapter 1 of Irwin Yalom's *Love's Executioner*, in which a young and gifted psychotherapist "falls victim" to an elderly female former patient and as a result finds it necessary to abandon his profession). These are the would-be heroes who take the wine offered by the princesses, become drugged, fall asleep, and then wake up to the sound of the executioner's blade-sharpening. One more often thinks of this happening in instances of sexual acting out by analysts with analysands, but the field of sleep also has its considerable hazards, not the least of which is feeding an already enlarged mother complex in the analyst with all its attendant symptoms of grandiosity and inflation.

To be honest, however, one must also admit that analysts can infect their analysands with psychic viruses as well. This often occurs with seemingly charismatic but actually dangerous analysts who actually consider it to be a "cure" when they see their analysands becoming more and more like themselves. What is happening usually is that their influence is creating a false persona without touching the underlying structures of the analysand's psyche. It would be wise to question this, at least, to avoid the inevitable disaster of a "transference cure."

When considering the phenomena of projection, of which transference is one type, the analyst must keep in mind that while the psychic virus with which infection begins is a foreign element and belongs to the analysand, every projection requires a "hook" to fasten on (von Franz 1980) and every projective identification needs a suitably rich "container" to house it (Grotstein 1981). Completely one-sided accounts in which either analyst or analysand is labeled as the "carrier" are clearly erroneous. In the analogy of the virus seeking entry into a host cell, there is the recognition that virus and host have something in common structurally—there must be a "fit"—in order for the infection to take place. The virus must search out a suitable host cell (i.e., complex) in the analyst's psychic body to fix upon and to enter.

In the case of William, the virus was clearly located within the mother complex. In his early history, he had been infected by his mother through their umbilical union. They never had become truly apart at the unconscious level of their union. William was still in symbiosis with a psychotic mother. What this had done to him was to block his individuation into masculine maturity. His psychic structures had remained amorphous and vague, and his ego complex could not extricate itself from the mother via identification with an available father.

Hence William had remained chronically stuck in the mother, not consciously identified with her but not separated from her either. The enlarged mother complex had so filled his psychic system that there was no room to grow an individuated ego complex. Most of his psychic life therefore took place underground within the unconscious. And one of the chief observable symptoms indicating this state of affairs was the narcoticlike field that William's own ego was trapped in, that is, his fuguelike dissociations. It was this that also communicated itself to me as analyst and infected me. I became nearly as sleepy and unmotivated as William was.

When William first met with me, he almost immediately infected me with this hypnotic, deadening force. His physical and psychological presence had a soporific effect on me. I hypothesize that the pathogenic virus entered my psyche via my mother complex, through a similarity in structure (although my own actual mother was quite different from his in many respects, she shared the trait of unconsciously undermining my separation from herself and my identifying with my father). Through this complex, the virus could enter and reproduce itself. Once inside my psychic body, this virus exaggerated those similar aspects in my mother complex, and as a consequence my ego very quickly felt the same stifling, smothering, hypnotic effect that William lived with continually. Thus the shamanic contact was made, and the circuit was closed.

In the course of the analysis, I became familiar with William's psychic structures through this infection, and I was able to observe his struggles to stay alive and sane directly from my own experience when in his presence. It was not the case that the hypnotic force was chiefly a defense on his ego's part against my intrusions or against his own psychic pain, but rather that we both fell into the same condition, both of us struggling to keep ourselves from falling into a state of possession and losing our minds by what could now be considered a mutual mother complex. At the core of this interactive field lay the Great Mother archetype in her containing, smothering, potentially castrating and devouring form. When our struggles to stay awake and to become conscious began to succeed, there was also support from another quarter: the dream of escaping from the grandmother's farm in the father's truck. This mobilization of individuation energy in a Hermes-the-thief trickster form, sufficient to escape the realm of the Great Mother, appeared in our work as a sort of divine intervention. The act of theft was transformational, as the trickster is meant to be (see Henderson 1967). And the paternal, spiritual aspect of the psyche was making itself available to William's fledgling ego in the image of a pickup truck. Perhaps this reflected the result of an incipient father transference to me.

The crisis that led to the conclusion of our analytical relationship was created by a source opposed to the Great Mother as well, namely William's sexuality. William had been drawn to the Church, largely by his Great Mother projection, and while I was seeing him he was also studying for a career in Her sanctuary. After our analytic work had reached the point of escaping from the Great Mother's realm (in the dream), William acted out sexually in such a way that he was banished from the Church: he was required to drop his studies and to remove himself from the Church's precincts. In other words, the Mother kicked him out. As a result, he was obliged to move to another part of the country for employment, and our analytic work came to a rather abrupt end. We were unprepared for this consciously, since it all took place within the course of one week, but the work that had been done to this point could sustain the break and be used for William's further growth and benefit.

Symbolically, the timing was good. William's ejection from Mother Church into the world of independent living, of work, and of freer interpersonal relationships would thrust him out of Paradise and require him to develop his autonomy and masculine standpoint in relation to the rest of the world. After he left the city, he telephoned me for a referral in his new location. I gave him the name of a male analyst, and he followed up on the referral by continuing analysis. It was this colleague who later reported to me that the work was going well and who showed no signs of experiencing the hypnotic field that I had found to be so potent. Perhaps William had truly escaped the force field of the Great Mother; perhaps the virus was no longer active; or perhaps the new analyst did not have a suitable receptor site.

After several months, I received a card from William thanking me for the help he had received in analysis and giving me some news of his present activities. I remember feeling pleased with the outcome, but I also noted to myself that William had not returned a book he once borrowed from a bookshelf in my office (Erich

Neumann's *The Origins and History of Consciousness)*. It is a book about the development of consciousness in Western culture through a release from the Great Mother cultures of the past into the presently waning but still dominant patriarchal form. I wondered if this book represented William's father's truck, as well as an extension of me and of our work. To myself, I hoped that this book—a vigorous statement by a keen and manly spirit—would continue to release an effective antidote against William's Great Mother virus and keep him on the path of psychological development toward maturity.

References

Dieckmann, H. 1991. *Methods in Analytical Psychology*. Wilmette, Ill.: Chiron Publications.

Grotstein, J. S. 1981. *Splitting and Projective Identification*. New York: Jason Aronson.

Grimm's Fairy Tales. 1972. New York: Random House.

Henderson, J. 1967. *Thresholds of Initiation*. Middletown, Conn.: Wesleyan University Press.

Jung, C. G. 1946. The psychology of the transference. In *CW* 16: 163–326. Princeton, N.J.: Princeton University Press, 1954.

Khan, M. 1986. In *Introduction to Holding and Interpretation* by D. W. Winnicott. Grove Press, 1987.

Ogden, T. H. 1989. *The Primitive Edge of Experience*. Northvale, N.J.: Jason Aronson.

Schwartz-Salant, N. 1989. *The Borderline Personality: Vision and Healing*. Wilmette, Ill.: Chiron Publications.

Stein, M. 1984. Power, shamanism, and maieutics in the countertransference. In *Transference/Countertransference,* N. Schwartz-Salant and M. Stein, eds. Wilmette, Ill.: Chiron Publications.

———. 1991. The muddle in analysis,. In *Liminality and Transitional Phenomena*, N. Schwartz-Salant and M. Stein, eds. Wilmette, Ill.: Chiron Publications.

von Franz, M.-L. 1980. *Projection and Re-Collection in Jungian Psychology*. La Salle, Ill.: Open Court.

Yalom, I. 1989. *Love's Executioner*. New York: Harper.

The Acoustic Vessel

Mary Lynn Kittelson

Analysis is a listening art. It takes place within a vessel sonorous with the mystery of the psyche. We are in constant inter-action with and through auditory energy, and in ways far more profound than most of us would guess. How odd then that we give so little conscious attention to the ear and to the experience of sound! As our most conscious sensory channel, vision guides our concep-tion of what psychic life is like: "seeing" means "understanding." However, Jung stated that images are "acoustic," "visual," and "feel-ing" (1926, par. 608), that some people are "visual types," some "audi-tory-verbal types," and some work best with their hands, with bodily movements, or automatic writing (1916, par. 170–171). Mostly, though, we work visually. Our words are heard primarily as content. We pay scant heed (consciously, at any rate) to how things sound.

Strong visual emphasis influences our attitudes and conclu-sions in ways we should be conscious of. In the phenomenology of seeing, there is a necessary distance between the seer and what is

Mary Lynn Kittelson is a Jungian analyst in private practice in St. Paul, Minnesota. She has master's degrees in English literature and psychology and trained as a Jungian analyst in Zurich, Switzerland. At present, she teaches and lectures on Jungian topics, dream and image work, animals in our souls, the American psyche, and auditory energy. She is the author of *Sounding the Soul: The Art of Listening*.

seen; the eyes naturally seek focus, a clear definition, such as where A is not B. Eye-minded consciousness assumes elements of distance and clarity. It must bring light, since it perceives through a transformation of the dark. Through the eye, the vibratory and participatory aspects of experience fall into the shadows. To be "ear-minded" is to be resonant, layered, slower, sensing things out before the light.

In dealing with the dim and dark, we are by no means bereft of our ears, nor, for that matter, our other senses. We need a broad range of image work styles, using many senses. An auditory style is more consonant with the findings of modern physicists, who have lent such stimulation and support to Jungian work. The eye's perceptive style, made of separateness and sharp differences, is no longer considered a scientifically accurate standpoint. Matter and energy are understood to be in constant, reciprocal vibration. Matter is inseparable from its "field," and it is the vibration of this field which is now studied, as well as the accompanying vibration of the scientific observer. Unlike light, whose vibratory nature is a less immediate experience, sound and silence reverberate in a palpable way; it is "natural" to work with them as an interactive field. "The world is more like music than matter," said a modern physicist (Andrews 1966).

What if we were to conceive of ourselves as primarily auditory beings within the analytic vessel? Our style would become more vibration-based, more layered and flowing. We would be in a more receptive interaction with the unconscious—not "bringing light" to it, but first being alive to it, such as it is.

Auditory Energy: Facts and Images

Sound in Our Lives

Our collective experience in modern society has supported auditory inattentiveness and misuse of sound. All too commonly, the sounds we hear are meaningless. Noise pollution is rampant. Sounds in the media and in public places are too much—too loud, too repetitious, too trivial, too shrill. We are victim to a cacophony of radio, TV, and video noise, and insipid, saccharine background Muzak. Verbal sound, we might assume, carries the most meaning. But we talk so much, and often so senselessly, so uselessly, in our culture, that it can be difficult to take the experience seriously. Blah-blah-blah! Sell-sell-sell! Chatter, complaint, jargon, interminable "how-to's," and the hyped-up headline style of broadcast news are so incessant, so frustrating, and often so upsetting, that we necessarily shut out differentiated response. As adults, we have lost our ear-minded center, which was vibrant in previous generations and remains so in much of infant and animal life. According to one neurolinguistic programing study,

> Most people in the U.S. do not actually hear the the sequence of words and the intonation patterns of what they, or other people, say. They are only aware of the pictures, feelings and internal dialogue that they have in response to what they hear. (Bandler and Grinder 1979, p. 124)

Audiologists warn that noise pollution not only causes literal hearing loss; it is also linked with ulcers, heart disease, low birth rates, birth defects—and psychoses and neuroses—to name just a few problems (Freese 1979, pp. 73-74). No wonder we do not better attend to auditory experience!

We may need more silence, but not soundlessness. Experiencing soundlessness is unnerving: most people report a sense of emptiness or deadness when subjected to a relatively soundproof room or to a sudden loss of hearing. Helen Keller, who was both deaf and blind, stated that deafness involved a loss worse than blindness (Freese 1979, p. 65). Deafness is associated with depression and paranoia (Kolb and Brodie 1982, p. 233). Operating outside of the deaf culture usually means significant difficulties in reception and self-expression. Worse, loss of hearing deprives us of our acoustic background—the humming, murmuring energy all around. A low level of sound is an animating container on which hearing people unconsciously depend.

For sound is healing. From the first squall of a newborn to the last rattle of breath leaving a dying person, sound expresses energy and life. As evidenced in the roots of the word *person* (and *personality* and *persona*), we "sound through" (Latin, *sonare* and *per*): the essential energy of sound vibrates at the center of our being. Sound is notably present in many creation myths. In the Judeo-Christian story, there is initially a state of darkness, formlessness, and emptiness. First it simply moves (kinetic energy); it becomes a creative force only when God speaks—only when this Spirit gets sounded— "Let there be light!" (Genesis 1:3). Sound comes before light and, in fact, brings light into being. The New Testament says "the Word" was in the beginning, being both with God and itself God (John 1:1-3). Jung noted this association of sound with creation in

Genesis, in two alchemy texts, and in a Greek papyrus (1912, par. 65).

The creation "story" of science, the Big Bang theory, also posits that the universe began with a spectacular noise, a monumental explosion. Science's ear is secular; there is no speech or intentionality in this creative sound. Yet this is indeed a great noise, this "big bang," lordly in its secular magnitude! It is a recurrent fundamental idea that sound comes first as a basic creative force. Then come light and vision. In Greek myth, too, there is a long association between healing and sound/music. Apollo gave the caduceus (the gift of healing) to Hermes after the latter's offering: the first lyre (the gift of music). Sound and healing exist in a well-established relationship of interchange.

In depth psychology, it seems that classical Freudians pay more heed to sound (see Schwaber 1980, Isakower 1939, Margulies 1985, and Reik 1948 and 1953). Perhaps this is due to their using the visually boring couch. In doing the work face to face, Jungians are more visually constellated. Jung focused on sound in only two areas, emphasizing its importance to each as a pathway to the unconscious. In his work on the Association Experiment, he noted that "by far the largest number of indirect associations" are a result of the complex indicator, *Klang* (Jung and Rilkin 1904, par. 88). However, it was on the subject of the "inner voice" (see Jung 1946, par. 308-323) that Jung waxed eloquent. He even advocated "talking back," thus the birth of the technique of active imagination. However, it is clear from his descriptions that Jung did not concentrate on the sound of voices, but on verbal content.

We might say auditory energy came to get Jung. It was the less conscious and more dramatic auditory events that reverberated in Jung's life. On two occasions, loud, inexplicable noises changed the direction of his life. In 1892, two such auditory shocks made him decide to choose psychology over other medical specialities (Jung 1965, pp. 105-107). Later, in 1909, two more such "reports" painfully reinforced his separation from Freud (ibid., pp. 155-156). In old age, Jung suffered auditory symptoms; he had otosclerosis, a condition common to old age which stiffens the middle ear joints. This condition resulted in repetitious noises inside his head, which he interpreted as making him listen to the inner world (Jung 1951, pp. 20-21). Jung's relationship to auditory energy seems to have been central and profound in his life, but largely unconscious.

Perhaps the typical "Jungian ear" at work resembles Jung's, with little auditory consciousness and an emphasis on the "audio-verbal." Jungian psychology attracts verbally articulate people, and many are easily seduced into a field replete with verbal virtuosity. Like a Siren Song, verbosity or verbal agility can seduce psychic voyagers from the real journey at hand. There is a temptation to gloss over the deeper, murkier, and more resonant elements of psychic life. Ear-based analytic work is primary in transforming talk-talk-talking into "the talking cure."

The Human Hearing Process

What is actually happening when hearing takes place? What are its facts and images? There are actually two main ways to hear. The first is conductive hearing. Whenever there is a sound, the air around its source begins to vibrate, to "bombard" or "caress" all of the body. This is a bit like being in a pool and feeling the agitation of the water. In conductive hearing, we hear through the whole body—skin, tissue, and in particular, bones (Joudry 1984, pp. 11, 119). Conductive hearing is highly interactive. It is also inescapable. There is no way to stop unwanted sounds; conductive sound is a given of the environment. We are simply subject to this level of auditory experience.

What we usually mean by "hearing" is the second type: neurosensory or selective hearing. Based on ear-to-brain messages, selective hearing focuses on a part of what is humanly audible, and registers this data in the brain as both conscious and subliminal information. Thus, in the analytic process, two kinds of auditory experience are always present. On one level, analysand and analyst are sounding directly into bone and skin, creating an inescapable bath of energy. On a second level, auditory energy vibrates into the complicated mechanisms of selective reception, where there are guiding auditory paths—indeed, veritable labyrinths. We need to maintain awareness of—and work from—some sense of the simultaneity and interchange of these two levels.

The pathways of hearing reverberate with overtones of the "Jungian" soul journey, echoing its images. Although all of the sensory processes are extraordinarily delicate and complicated, auditory perception reveals a participatory style of consciousness. Ear work means interactivity—perceptible vibratory contact within mutually vibrating surroundings.

The journey of auditory energy begins when sound waves

enter flesh-covered, shell-shaped outer ears. The receptive, cupped shape of the ear guides the sound into the ear canal; as it narrows, it amplifies the sound on its way to the eardrum (Freese 1979, pp. 15–16). Sound energy has entered human materiality—flesh and cartilage. It has "incarnated" and begun moving along the path of "mattering." This is the first of three transformations: mechanical energy moves from air into body, into matter.

There are four tiny eardrums, a minute inner drumming, in every analytic hour. The eardrum, about one-third of an inch in diameter, is so sensitive that it can "hear" a depression of the eardrum of less than one half-billionth of an inch. Auditory stimuli during any one millisecond number in the hundreds of thousands. The eardrum further amplifies the sound and channels it into the middle ear, which is about three-sixteenths by three-eighths of an inch. Here, it travels along three small interconnecting bones: the hammer (malleus), anvil (incus), and stirrup (stapes). These further amplify the sound about a hundred times. The minute foot of the stirrup fits into what is termed, elegantly enough, the oval window. Twenty-five times smaller than the eardrum, it further amplifies the sound and provides the transition into the watery labyrinth of the inner ear (Freese 1979, pp. 16–18, 28).

The inner ear, the inner chamber, is full of mystery. Unseen, it is set about one and a half inches into the head on each side. The foot of the stirrup functions like a piston, pressing into the cochlea, which is a closed, fluid-filled tube, curled up like a snail. Since the cochlea has rigid, bony walls, the vibrating stirrup foot creates pressure waves in the cochlear fluid. It is the amazing task of the inner ear to transform mechanical energy (the moving of flesh, bone, and cartilage) into hydraulic pressure waves (Freese 1979, pp. 16–18, 31). This is the second transformation, into a watery inner world.

The cochlea, about the size of a little fingertip, is actually made up of two spirals within one, one bony and one membranous. The cochlea is known as "the labyrinth." Audiologists note that "the organ of hearing is in the labyrinth" (Freese 1979, pp 18–19): the organic center of hearing is an inner, labyrinthine, watery depth. Within the cochlea, about seventeen thousand minute acoustic hair cells, together known as the Organ of Corti, move in response to the auditory waves in the fluid. They differentiate and analyze both the sounds we are conscious of and each tone's unconsciously registered overtone series. These tiny movements produce electrochemical changes, exciting the eighth cranial (or acoustic) nerve, which then sends messages to the interpreting brain (Freese 1979, pp. 19-21, 34). This is the third transformation, from a watery world into the electrochemical brain.

It is a lively, sparked pathway to the brain. A series of coded signals, the neural impulses, race through the brain, firing at the rate of a thousand messages each second. The auditory process can distinguish time differences of between six and twelve millionths of a second (Freese 1979, pp. 39, 52). Hearing now enters the realm of electrochemistry, where matter and energy meet. The neural world describes a play of positive/negative charges, the interaction of which in atomic and subatomic physical particles produces the different forms of matter, and the interplay of which in Jungian psychology produces psychic differentiation. Audiology, neurology, and Jungian psychology all speak of analysis, differentiation, and interpretation.

The semicircular canals, also located in the inner ear, are the organ of balance, another central Jungian concept. Like the cochlea, they also consist of a fluid-filled double spiral or labyrinth. Head movements—up or down, right or left, and back and forth—are registered by means of the tiny hair cells within (Freese 1979, pp. 21-22, 36-37). The human auditory process offers a wealth of evocative facts and images.

The Acoustic Vessel

What are some of the ways to become more conscious of auditory energy and work with it within the acoustic vessel of analytic work? A few possibilities, with case examples, follow.

Initial Contact

Like God's voice in Genesis, the opening tones of an analysis sound forth, setting things into motion. For most analysands and analysts, initial contact is made by telephone, a purely auditory process. Such a call is often full of energy, since initiating analysis often indicates much thought, emotion, and trouble. When the analyst picks up the ringing receiver, there is a new voice, a new line sounding—sounding him or her out—from the first moment. This is the first perception of the potential partner, received on an auditory wavelength. Each partner begins a movement toward the energic realities of the other. Consciously or not, they join in an experience of tone, meter, pitch, and melody; they complement, oppose, echo each other in an auditory reciprocity. This "duet" is the real beginning of the work.

For example, in one such initial contact, I asked for an appointment with an unknown analyst. I was full of anxious anticipation. Amid my hesitant yet constantly catching-up tones and rhythms, the analyst, to my ear, suddenly sang out:

Let's / Take a **chance!**

This phrase, resounding in my head, was like the first strains of a waltz. It sounded firm, engaging, and somehow old-fashioned, too. This proved an apt image in retrospect, for our ensuing work did indeed begin in a whirl; and—to my amazement—he led with some firmly structuring steps. My acoustic fantasy had proved meaningful.

Such moments are like a prelude or an overture. And what will follow? a few desultory phrases? a brief melody? a song in blues style? a jazz improvisation? or an entire opera? What kinds of instrumentation, accents, meter, and echo will emerge? Whatever happens, it is yet to be heard.

Rhythm and Return

Rhythm is a constant and vital part of our lives. It takes place in the meter of our hearts, in our breaths, our footfalls, in all of the leavings and returnings of our lives. The throbbing and beeps and clicks of machines make up the pulse of our minutes and hours and days. There are also larger rhythms: day and night, weather and seasons turning, the moon and planets and stars as they make their rounds in space and time. Rhythm is a subtly powerful force, in the session and out. We are probably most aware of its moment-to-moment revelations, but it functions most importantly as shape and structure, as a meaningful pattern of going out and returning.

Every hour is shaped by its ritual sounds. Some are common to every hour, like the bell or buzzer, or the door swishing open and closed. Some are important to certain seasons or periods of the work, like the stamping of snow boots or the zipping of the art portfolio. They form a natural part of the "ceremony" of soul work, not unlike the liturgical year observed in the cycle of the Christian church.

Rhythm, in both its regularity and its shifts of emphasis, usually focuses and facilitates awareness; it prevents experience from being lost in a sea of samenesses.[1] Rhythm provides a matrix of importance; psychic processes take on a "soundness," as meaningful curves, waves, phases emerge. An analysand usually has a rhythmic pattern. The usual way he or she places emotions, ideas, sounds, movements, and images within the pattern of the hour gives each a felt "weight." An atypical rhythmic pattern draws added attention; the sensed changes, the absences and additions, make us take note. If a usually brisk woman shuffles unevenly to her chair and sits humped in a throbbing silence, a new attentiveness is called for. There is a need for keen (if silent) reaction, just as an animal, vibrating with acuity, pricks its ears in the dark.

One common way we experience an auditory pattern is the crescendo, a rising to a climax. For some analysands, this moment of highest intensity occurs at approximately the same moment in most sessions, e.g., ten minutes before the end. As in an effective theatrical or musical piece, only when a solid structure has been laid underneath to take the load of the "big moment" can the top of the crescendo, the climax, be accomplished. Where and how this intensity is placed is important to the experience of its impact. Perhaps it has been ground away at, or rushed into; or maybe it has suddenly descended or has slowly, almost imperceptibly, ripened. How the work proceeds rhythmically is part of its meaning.

To my ear, "sensing out" an analysand's connection to what he or she is saying is often based on rhythmic aspects. What we call "vibes" or "intuition" or "a feeling" may well be imaged as acoustic, or even musical. Perhaps an analysand slugs through a story with pistonlike inevitability or is always rushing forward and then getting stuck. Such rhythms offer images (both auditory and kinesthetic), and thus offer experience and insight as to how that analysand is responding to his or her own psychic realities. An attentive ear can help the analysand to hear such basic patterns—and their changes—in relation to inner and outer life. The rhythmic pattern may express the client's relationship to the analytic process or to material currently vibrant, to a certain complex or archetypal field. It might have overtones from past or future. The rhythm is also part of the transference/countertransference field. It is interactive with the analyst, like a duet, in part responding to that analyst's own idiosyncratic working style.

Elements of rhythm provide especially clear clues regarding the type, degree, and pattern of defenses that an analysand—as well as an analyst—is using. Perhaps the sense is of an accelerating flight forward or an irregular sidestep, a sudden muffle or flatfall or a silence moving backward; there may be panicky galloping at the margins of issues, or there may be a perceived absence of rhythm, a "stuckness," in one of the myriad ways that can occur. Such perceptions can be brought into the hour as images and offered for reexperience and working through. As vibrant recall, they deepen the experience. And they may well echo on.

Patterns, I suppose, are most necessary when orientation is difficult. In my sessions with one analysand, a twenty-three-year-old Austrian woman, I often became lost in a fog. Her content was disconnected, and convoluted, her manner furtive, and there were long, vague silences. She spoke only sporadically, and her eye contact was minimal. Next to this smoke screen of diffuseness, it provided welcome orientation to focus on her auditory pattern.

The rhythmic pattern of this woman's sessions was as fixed as the stroke of a metronome; my first thought was how strongly it compensated for her diffuseness. As time passed, the pattern became more definite. Beginnings were somewhat chaotic; she might mention in a rush the content of what would become "the main business of the hour" in a light patter of small talk, or else in a loud, sudden "flashing" often accompanied by a sharp slap to her thigh. This was the percussive prelude of things to come. As more intense contact ensued, more erratic-sounding speech would occur, with longer silences, which seemed to be busy times for her. Any attempt on my part to ask about or echo an earlier theme—even at the softest volume or the lowest and slowest of tones—was either sharply or, more often, very dully rebuffed. It was clear I was simply to be there, since any move on my part, however slight, was met with upset or withdrawal. She controlled me as rigidly as she controlled the hour. Usually, this "main business" came back suddenly about three minutes from the end, often after a pointed glance at the clock. BAM! This was her "climax point." She would strike and then retreat. She initiated cutting off her sessions on the stroke, like an executioner, every hour, leaving things, and herself and me as well, in an outspilling turmoil. We were caught in a rigid/diffuse conflict, chronically sabotaged at the end.

Becoming conscious of this difficult rhythm, this machinelike "unsuccess," brought more clarity to my confused reactions. It offered meaning and shape to how she was using the hour. I felt subjected to this pattern; nothing I did, or did not do, could change it. To her ear, describing or confronting it clearly caused unbearable confusion and criticism. Over time, exactly this rigid pattern was her clearest communication. We together had to experience, again and again, this prisonlike rigidity, this vague but heavy impossibility, which was apparently her experience of human contact all along. The only difference was our growing clarity about it.

In this diffuse and tortured field, I was "tested," hour after hour; I had to be ready to try to "catch" and hold what she would so reliably drop, and I failed again and again. In being so subjected, like her, to the field, I could feel the lostness. It took a long twenty months for enough ground to form under us in our struggles; then she moved, in an oddly quiet yet dramatic slide, into a space of noticeably more trust. The fifty-seven-minute climax all but disappeared. Her rhythm became a more flexible phenomenon which not only allowed, but sometimes sought and even demanded, that she be heard and resonated to with enough space and time—within the hour. The ways that this woman "shaped" her sessions rhythmically had offered communication and meaning.

Sound Synchronicity

In analytic work, sound synchronicity usually occurs in the form of sound that enters the hour unexpectedly, such as happenings in the building, sounds of traffic, sirens, animals and insects, the weather, things falling or breaking, or some involuntary body sounds. Unthinking, we may ignore many such sounds. From an ego standpoint, they sound interruptive. But, as Jung remarked in a letter, "In a quite irrational way we must be able to listen also to the voice of nature, thunder for instance, even if this means breaking the continuity of consciousness" (1951, p. 21).

Since maintaining a sense of quiet and protection in the vessel is important, it can be a surprise to discover how often these "noises from the outside" contribute to the work. There can be meaning in their timing, in the unique ways they make us experience things, and wonder and ponder. While subtle synchronistic events are easily missed, recurrent or loud ones are inescapable. During one long phase with an analysand, the body therapy group meeting upstairs would sometimes begin thumping, stamping, pounding, and hee-hawing their way into our sessions. This was noteworthy not only because this group was usually quiet, but also because their sounds, which occurred in no other analysands' hours, followed us through three different schedule changes over two years. The thumping and hee-hawing would typically assert themselves at moments when she seemed numb, having receded into remote silence. From my side, any attempt to "help" only made her recede farther. We were, repeatedly and resoundingly, stuck. We began calling these sounds "devil-noises." I think we needed their nasty disruptions—to shake her out of numbed rejection of her own emotional reality, which was indeed "devilish."

This woman reported being actively scoffed at in her family for any emotional need or anger. She had internalized these attitudes, disregarding or scoffing at others' emotions while maintaining a romanticized view of her "warm, close" family. This hee-hawing and thumping from above, from the distanced and arrogant ceiling of her own dismissive, superior attitudes, were recurrent synchronistic events, dramatizing and stimulating the energies bursting to be recognized amid so much frustration. Actually, dramatic synchronistic events were frequent in her life. Such "outside attacks" were apparently channels of volatile interactivity with her own walled-off inner violence.

These sounds did finally "release" us. Interestingly enough, they stopped at approximately the same time that the analysand began risking more clarity about her hurt feelings and the aggressive, arrogant feelings she felt toward me and others. The work now shifted to the human-to-human channel, with a slower and more mediating exchange of energies; I then became the focus for acknowledging and confronting these formidable shadow sides.

Echo and Return

Pat Berry, who has also written on the "poisoned ear" of King Hamlet, speaks of the importance of echo. She says that a deepening echo, one that completes the word to itself, is what psychological understanding is all about (1979, p. 120). People constantly echo themselves, others, and even objects, re-calling and re-questing deepening contact through words and tones and silences. We "play it again" to hear it, to experience it once again. Echoes can also shift meaning. They reposition, calling up other places and times still vibrant, re-sounding them to consciousness again.

It is important to clarify from the start that I am speaking of "echoing" in its specifically acoustic sense: I mean holding to the integrity of the sound in what has been expressed. People also use this term to mean restating a client's ideas or feelings back to him, with no particular care for its original auditory form. This is already a change or reworking of the acoustic communication; it is not a faithful echo, for the person's original auditory image has been lost. In a genuine echoing process, the analyst keeps to the sounds, the exact words, as originally expressed. That analyst holds true to the melody, timbre, meter, and rhythm, recalling the original moment in a resonant way. The analyst assists the image's telling nature. The sense within the vessel is calling back, and calling back, and calling back.

Echo is everywhere, whether we emphasize her malignant side ("neurotic patterns," "echolalia," or "obsessive/compulsive disorder"), or her constructive side ("role modeling," "ritual," or "circumambulation"). Often an echo sounds as if it has a drive of its own. Begun as simple repetition, an echo suddenly startles. In nature, echoes are trickiest when they ventriloquize our sounds back to us; we suddenly discover ourselves at a surprising new angle in relation to our own sounds. Subjectively, we are in some different space because of how those sounds have resounded us! Echoes fascinate, calling to us in an ongoing resonant interplay. We listen and linger on the cliff edge, at the cave opening, as in analysis.

Visual "mirroring" and acoustic "echoing" are closely related phenomena, each with its own phenomenology. These two modalities, the auditory and visual, appear as a dramatic couple—alas, a doomed one—in the Greek myth of Echo and Narcissus. Analyst and analysand are also a pair of matched/mismatched seekers in high-energy, reverberating exchange. Like the grottoes and caves, the consulting room is an acoustic vessel that contains longing, dreams, loneliness, pain, and poignant search. Potentiality is the essence, never satisfied. The feeling tone is longing, demand; there is denial, frustration, perplexity—and ever more longing. This is not so much pathology, and in a way, not even tragedy. It is very much a given of human existence, and is poignantly felt in analytic work. This myth beautifully evokes the longing, the "togetherness" and "separateness" in relating, to oneself and to others.

In Ovid's *Metamorphoses,* in this ear-minded poetic space, this echoing quest rings profound. In analysis, the resonant, newly positioned words and sounds, ideas and thoughts, feelings and silences express the call between our substantial and insubstantial, soulful selves. This longing holds us to the task, even when, wearied by cursedness and desperation, we cannot see a thing. For it is by no means a given that Echo's energy—her longing, her passion, and her highly tenacious demands—will be well received. Echoes, disturbing and tricky, often carry a confusing mix of chatter and profundity. Perhaps staying with Echo means staying with echo, since her very essence is resonance, resoundingness. But, it is tricky; things in Echo's realm are catchy, permeable, back-and-forth. An analyst too wary of participatory energy, of too much "inter" in the "activity," will feel contaminated.

Echo's cursedness, her "stuckness" and useless persistence, suggest not only her pathology but, interactively, a bored ear. The mythic image of echo suggests a potential for resonance in a way that "neurosis" or "mindless parroting" does not. As is clear from the myth, whose ears hear, and how, matters a great deal. In Ovid's text, Echo's echoing is full of meaning; in his story, he evokes the kind of listening that poignantly discovers the significance in Echo's sounds. Analysts must have ears trained by poets like Ovid—the ears to hear.

There is the familiar echo of overidentification or "possession." Something begins to be heard as echo, such as "just what my father always said," or "just the tone my mother used to use." It is an old, old strain. There are also cultural and subcultural echoes, which resound oddly in a time and space alien to them. Echoing out of time or out of place, out of a different culture, out of different geographical areas—as male or female, old or young, sacred or profane—all these carry meaning.

The most conscious auditory experience for most people is music. An echo experience commonly arrives in the form of a song, running on and on in the ear. These are the singsong offerings of the psyche. Noting and "singing along" can be vital. We are used to taking little care with sound, so it is easy to be oversimplistic. Meaning might lie in lyrics or in the sounds themselves (the rhythm, melody, or timbre), and most likely in both. It might also be tied to the memory field around the song. Auditory images are difficult to hold; it takes more effort to do the kind of many-layered image work than with a more "stoppable" visual image. A musical approach is very helpful (see Arye 1987).[2]

Just like the nymph Echo, many echoes excel in persistence. The following story illustrates how echo persisted over one short session. A Swiss woman in her forties dreamed that, amid warnings, she was supposed to go back to a certain area to bring food for her mother and her invalid grandmother. As we worked with this dream, the word *invalid* began taking on echo, as if it had its own life. It rang oddly, persistently. *Invalid* at first meant "crippled," eliciting sympathy and care for these mother figures. As it echoed on, it slipped into the realm of her college course on psychological test-ing. Now it had shifted to the realm of validity; her mother figures had become "invalid."[3] They now sounded unreliable, no longer valid in her life. For this overdependent woman, who had such trou-ble saying no to her mother, this tricky echo had pulled her first into binding sympathy; then it had shifted, tricking her at least for a moment into hearing her mother figures' invalidity in her life.

Sometimes an echo is less a visiting entity than a quality, a sense of resonance around things. A "sense of echo" is present, one that is its own experience. In her essay, "Echo's Passion," Pat Berry offered some images of echo as a quality: "Some things echo empty (like a Pinter play), some things echo overfull (like a heavily sym-bolic poem), some things echo flat and then big (like melodrama), and some things echo not at all—like jargon, say, or interpretation" (1979, p. 120). Catching fantasies around echo makes experience clearer and may invite further image work.

Interpretation, says Berry, echoes not at all. Nonresonant inter-pretation, and I would add, archetypal amplification, might mean the analyst has "abandoned" that space of acoustically based seeking together. What is often understood as resistance to the content of an interpretation may be resistance to the analyst's talking at the analysand from too separate and nonvibrant a distance, in a basically "narcissistic" way. If interpretation is heard to stop the longing, stop the "call," then interpretation indeed does not echo. However, the Latin roots of *interpret* describe the action of placing (*pretere*) be-tween (*inter*). An interpretation can be "placed between" the analysand and analyst in a less than conclusive, more poetic, echoic way. It then becomes a resounding new image placed among the existing ones. And, one effective way to keep this sense of call and mystery in interpreting is to stay in contact with the acoustic im-agery, as in a poem or song. The analyst literally echoes, just like Echo. Each new interpretation becomes a stanza in a ballad while the original interpretation emerges like a refrain, always returned to from a new angle as the verses unfold. Tempo and timing are two other great lessons of the auditory realm.

Final Comments

There is no space to touch on the many other possible areas, for example, simultaneity and flow, sound accent, symbolic and po-etic listening, musical accompaniment, auditory imagery in dreams, voices inside and out (see Bliss 1983), hearing what is not said, hearing silence (see Federer 1989), pre- and nonverbal work, hearing in early life, and sensory channel "typology."

A few final remarks: in working with auditory images, the level of vulnerability might be high. The inescapability of sound and relative absence of boundaries in the auditory field demand care in pacing and style as well as constant checking. The level of consciousness is apt to be very low. Early developmental levels may be constellated, because hearing is especially important in early infant, and even fetal, life. A person's "sensory typology" affects his or her ability to work well with auditory images, as well as his or her level of ear training.

Certain types of cases probably require auditory work. It is invaluable in working with the nonverbal or preverbal level, whether animal or infant or even fetal. Lastly, it is vital for people fixated, say, in a wounding auditory aggression or chaos or emptiness as part of a complex field or developmental level. Considerable auditory sensitivity is vital; for such a client, almost any talk will be a poisoned base of reception, no matter how verbally accurate or skilled the analyst. If verbal listening cannot occur, "the talking cure" has no chance.

In this time of "psycho-babble" and alleged cost-effectiveness, it is more difficult, and also more necessary, to listen well and to "sound the depths." Psychic energy, like a rich musical composition, strikes the ear in a moving simultaneity of levels. Words and statements, like musical motifs, vibrate out more clearly with each hearing. A listener begins to "understand" on listening again, both inside and out, just as with a piece of music. It takes time, as well as interest and experience, to hear the psyche well. We then "play back" what has been played to us and also on us by an analysand in an interactive field. We are sounding boards, helping sound that person back to his or her central truths.

Notes

1. This is not to say that rhythm always assists in finding meaning; it can also detract from or dull consciousness. A rhythmically singsong voice or a machinelike (mindless) repetition has an irritating or numbing effect; it defends against the psychological impact of that moment.

2. Both process-oriented psychology and neurolinguistic programming provide valuable training in sensory channel awareness and, sometimes, ideas for working further.

3. To be auditorily accurate, I should mention that in German the two meanings of *invalid* are stressed on the same syllable.

References

Andrews, D. P., 1966. In *The Magic of Tone and the Art of Music,* D. Rudhyar, ed. Boulder, Colo.: Shambhala, 1982.

Arye, L. 1987. Process-oriented seminar "Working with Music and Sound," Nov. 19, Zurich, Switzerland.

———. 1988. Music the messenger. Dissertation. Antioch University.

Bandler, R., and J. Grinder. 1979. *Frogs into Princes: Neurolinguistic Programming.* Moab, Utah: Real People Press.

Berry, P. 1979. Echo's passion. In *Echo's Subtle Body.* Dallas: Spring Publications, 1982.

Bliss, B. 1983. The singer and the voice. Diploma thesis, C. G. Jung Institute, Zurich, Switzerland.

Federer, Y. 1989. Silence: Nonverbal aspects of analytical psychology. Diploma thesis, C. G. Jung Institute, Zurich, Switzerland.

Freese, A. S. 1979. *You and Your Hearing.* New York: Charles Scribner's Sons.

Isakower, O. 1939. On the exceptional position of the auditory sphere. *International Journal of Psychoanalysis* 20:340-348.

Joudry, P. 1984. *Sound Therapy and the Walk Man.* St. Denis, Sask.: Steele and Steele.

Jung, C. G. 1912. The hymn of creation. In *CW* 5:56-114. Princeton, N.J.: Princeton University Press, 1956.

———. 1916. The transcendent function. In *CW* 8:131-193. Princeton, N. J.: Princeton University Press, 1969.

———. 1926. Spirit and life. In *CW* 8:601-648. Princeton, N. J.: Princeton University Press, 1969.

———. 1946. The development of personality. In *CW* 17:284-323. Princeton: Princeton University Press, 1954.

———. 1951. Letter to "Dr. S." (Aug. 8, 1951). *C. G. Jung Letters*, vol. 2. G. Adler and A. Jaffe, eds.; R. F. C. Hull, trans. Princeton, N.J.: Princeton University Press, 1973.

———. 1965. *Memories, Dreams, Reflections.* A. Jaffe, ed.; R. Winston and C. Winston, trans. New York: Random House.

Jung, C. G. and Rilkin, F. 1904. The associations of normal subjects. In *CW* 2:3-495. Princeton, N.J.: Princeton University Press, 1973.

Kolb, L., and Brodie, H. K. H. 1982. *Modern Clinical Psychology.* 10th ed. Philadelphia: W. B. Saunders.

Margulies, A. 1985. On listening to a dream: The sensory dimensions. *Psychiatry* 48:371-381.

Ovid. *Selected Works.* J. C. Thornton and M. J. Thornton, eds. London: J. M. Dent & Sons, 1939, 180-189.

Reik, T. 1948. *Listening with the Third Ear: The Inner Experience of a Psychoanalyst.* New York: Grove Press, 1975.

———. 1953. *The Haunting Melody: Psychoanalytic Experiences in Life and Music.* New York: Grove Press.

Schwaber, E. 1980. A particular perspective on analytic listening. *Journal of the American Psycho-analytic Association*, 519-546.

Analysis and Erotic Energies

Pamela Donleavy

Dr. Robert Stein's[1] article "The Fear of the Phallos" (1991) raises several important issues that I find are key to the healing of some of the psyche's deepest wounds. In discussing the theories that Peter Rutter expressed in *Sex in the Forbidden Zone* (1989),[2] Stein criticizes Rutter for failing to adequately deal with the erotic and transformative energies of Pan, the phallic God, when this energy becomes manifest in the psyche as the experience of the Pan/nymph primal chase. I, too, find Rutter's theories lacking, and filled with a patriarchal fear of phallos and the dark, erotic feminine. Since I believe that the energies within this primal scene are energies that underlie one of the most profound creative experiences, the *coniunctio*, I would like to offer a different perspective on the subject and propose a structure for transformation as well as healing when the primal erotic energies are constellated.

Pamela Donleavy, J.D., is a candidate-in-training at the C. G. Jung Institute in Boston and a practicing mental health counselor and psychotherapist in Newtonville, Massachusetts. She is a former Assistant District Attorney and Special Assistant United States Attorney in Philadelphia and the former president of the C. G. Jung Foundation of the Delaware Valley.

The Pan/Nymph Energies

This writer is only too familiar with the terror of the nymph, the energy that can turn me into a focused predator, and the intrapsychic experience where I am the woman fleeing the ever-threatening rapist. These intense experiences may emerge at any point in the life process of individuals: during interpersonal relationships, during the creative process, and even while they sleep.

Pan/nymph energy races through our psyches, possesses our egos, and blocks our development. Until some transformation of the energy occurs, behavior will be conditioned through a type of repetition compulsion, stultifying our creativity, and condemning us to deaden our souls or to act in ways that give us only temporary relief. Although life itself presents us with the opportunity to work on this energy, the analytic setting can provide a safe and structured environment to isolate this energy, learn what it is trying to tell us, and transform it at its source.

When the analytic hour becomes erotically charged, the primal Pan/nymph energies have appeared. Depending upon the state of the mind/body split of the individuals involved, this energy may be felt within the psyche and bodies of each, as well as in the field between and around the analytic couple. This energy may arise in a number of ways, for example, analyst as Pan/analysand as nymph; analysand as Pan/analyst as nymph, or masculine psyche as Pan/feminine psyche as nymph.

This latter configuration may occur intrapsychically and interpsychically. Interpsychic interplay of the Pan/nymph energies may be doubled if the intrapsychic masculine/feminine development of the individuals in the analytic couple is both unequal and a mirror image of the other person. Indications of interpsychic "doubling" may be experienced when each party wishes to seduce and be seduced, victimize and be victimized, rape and be raped. When these feelings arise, multiples of the interpsychic Pan/nymph energies have been constellated.

Whether one or multiple Pan/nymph energies have arisen, the transformation process will be the same. The primal chase must first be stopped, and change on each side of the Pan/nymph split must occur. Each side can be viewed separately. However, development of one will cause a reaction in the other. Their destinies are intertwined, for better or for worse.

The Approach to a *Coniunctio*

In *Sex in the Forbidden Zone* (1989), Rutter details his near sexual encounter with a patient, Mia, whom he describes as a seductive and troubled woman. His account is a wonderful description of the approach to a *coniunctio*. Unfortunately, Rutter perceives this encounter as an approach to literal sex in the forbidden zone. His conscious labeling of it as such and his reaction to it aborted the process, and a lesser healing occurred. I quote his narrative of this encounter in detail, since I use his experience for descriptive purposes throughout this article.

Rutter describes how Mia, during one of her sessions, slid off her chair onto the floor and sat cross-legged in front of him. Rutter details how her sexual posturing grew more intense as she looked up at him pleadingly, wondering through her tears whether men would always use her and throw her away. Mia then edged her way towards Rutter, brushing her breasts against his legs, and began to bury her head in his lap. Rutter theorizes that Mia "inexorably reenacted her familiar role as sexual victim," and that all she needed to complete this role was Rutter's participation.

Rutter describes his feelings as being an "intoxicating mixture of timeless freedom" stemming from the "illusion of such moments in which a man can convince himself that nothing but sexual merger with the female body and spirit seems real." He states that "he felt all at once extremely powerful—and very, very vulnerable."

Rutter asked Mia to return to her chair. She did so without hesitation. In their respective seats, they began a therapeutic exploration of Mia's self-destructive pattern. Rutter describes this near-miss with entering the forbidden zone as a "healing moment." (Rutter 1989, pp. 3–5).

I view Mia's approach to Rutter as wishing to seduce and be seduced. This aroused a comparable feeling in her analyst partner: the erotic phallic sense of power, and the vulnerable feminine desire to be seduced that he described. The desire to act out sexually, a literal merger of masculine and feminine energies, emerged from the constellation of the Pan/nymph energies between Rutter's masculine side and Mia's feminine side, and the Pan/nymph energies between Mia's masculine side and Rutter's feminine side. The intrapsychic imbalance of each individual locked in interpsychically. The seductive female has a predator for an animus, and a male analyst who has not consciously incorporated the erotic, dark feminine side of his anima will be extremely vulnerable to this unconscious attack.

The erotic desire for merger is the first indication that the individual has a psychic split that needs to be healed. The desire for wholeness has been ignited but directly conflicts with all the original reasons that first caused the split to occur. Therefore, the task in analysis is to hold the tension until the healing image, experience, or synchronous event occurs that will bring what is unconscious into consciousness. Failure to do this, whether through avoidance or through acting out, merely sets up a repetition compulsion that will eventually be reenacted. With either choice, the unconscious psychic part that was experienced through the desire or the fear stays still within the unconscious.[3] If the tension can be held, and the psychic part made conscious in each person, the couple will feel not an overwhelming need for physical merger, but a psychic resonance between them. This resonance will also be experienced as a new intrapsychic wholeness.

Rutter's conscious matrix did not include this possibility. Therefore he had no tools to do anything other than what he did. Mia's unconsciousness of what her desires really meant moved her to try to literalize merger with the other.

When the analytic couple can view erotic energy as a possible opening for psychic transformation and greater wholeness, the stage may be set for a profound healing. Therefore, I suggest several constructs that can be included in the conscious matrix that should help hold the tension and help one wait for healing of the unconscious split.

Stopping the Pan/Nymph Chase

First, Pan needs to become conscious of the results of his unlimited desire. Pan's unrestrained desire leads to the rape and death of the very thing he desires, thereby creating in him an eternal, insatiable desire with nothing left to fill it. This thing may be innocence—which needs to be realized and protected, not raped and destroyed. Initially, Pan needs conscious limits to his desire.

The nymph must stop running and hiding, trying to elude Phallos. She must learn to stop the action, stop running, and ask Phallos what it is he wants of her. Similarly, Jung described a patient's repetitive dream in which he was being chased by a lion. Finally, one night the man stopped in the dream, turned to the lion, and asked,

"What is it you want of me?" The lion responded that he had been chasing the dreamer to give him a message from God.

The nymph must also find the strength, courage, and wisdom to do this, knowing full well that any number of things may occur, ranging from annihilation to *coniunctio*. In terms of feminine personifications, the nymph needs to find the strength of Lilith,[4] and the wisdom of Sophia,[5] as well as to embody the transformative power of Aphrodite[6] to stop and face the phallic power of Pan.

Two current books are helpful for this stage of the Pan/nymph development. *Iron John*, by Robert Bly (1990), gives considerable insight into restraining and integrating the Pan energies. *Leaving My Father's House*, by Marion Woodman (1992), outlines three paths of feminine development, detailing the importance of strengthening the feminine vessel so that it will not shatter under the force of the creative phallic thrust.[7]

Each book also shows the importance of confronting the incest issues that must be overcome to reach the *coniunctio* promised at the end of each protagonist's journey, which end is marriage to the princess or king, respectively. The protagonist in *Iron John* must steal the key to Iron John's cage (the instinctual masculine) from under his mother's pillow. The protagonist in the fairy tale underlying *Leaving My Father's House* must flee her father's house to avoid an incestuous marriage to him.

As Robert Stein has so eloquently expressed in his book, *Incest and Human Love* (1984), the wounds of incest in the feminine and masculine psyche must be healed before the mind/body, sexual/spiritual split can be united. *Iron John* and *Leaving My Father's House* show the determination and commitment required to heal and make conscious the parental incest wounds. Only after the masculine and feminine sides of the psyche have dealt with the mind/body, spiritual/sexual split caused by the parental incest wounds can the ultimate brother/sister sacred *coniunctio* be approached. For me, the healing of the parental incest wound was the most difficult. This occurred for me during analysis, and what follows is a brief account of my experience.

Healing the Father/Daughter Incest Split: A Personal Account

I chose my analyst because I had an erotic transference to him. At the time, I knew little of Jungian theory and nothing about

psychic splits. I had, however, experienced a series of ill-fated relationships with older, married, or clerical men, and I felt it was time
to work on the transference reaction directly, in a safe environment.
I informed my analyst of this in our first session and he agreed.

For the first two months, I shared my story, and there was a
feeling of apprehension as the ego and unconscious of each of us
tested the waters. In the third month, I was telling him of a recent
award I had received, how honored and excited I was, but how I
also felt extremely empty as well. He responded very compassion-
ately, and I felt warmth grow around and between us. He then
pulled back, as if snapping out of a daze, and accused me of seducing him. I felt the warmth abruptly leave me. I told him that I hadn't
felt him enter me, but I felt him pull out. The withdrawal left me inflamed and confused. I felt an almost unbearable desire for him. He
too was shaken.[8]

During the ensuing week, I fought my desire. I did not intend
to let this happen to myself again. The next week, I learned that his
wife was dying of cancer; three weeks later, she died. Since my
mother had died of cancer at the age of fifty-two, I was suddenly
thrown back into that pain and terror of disease and loss. My body
was tortured. Every cell ached. It was excruciating. Then, the fight
left me; I collapsed into the situation. I gave myself to it and prayed
for guidance.

My analyst was gone for two weeks, and returned clearly devas-
tated by his loss. As I watched his suffering, I felt the most incredible healing energy arise from deep within me, an energy I hadn't
felt before. I couldn't bear his pain; something in me wanted to heal
it. This energy would best be described as a deep, feminine, nurturing energy, an energy that had previously been foreign to me. It had
never been available to me for my own wounds, but arose on its
own in response to his.

How he was able to tend to his patients and bear the pain of
his loss is unknown to me. It was valiant and I felt privileged to witness it. He walked the line with me between acknowledging the
erotic field between us and maintaining a working analytic vessel.
My experience aided me as well. I had known the sacred in past relationships and had chosen to fall into sacrilege. The pain of that
sacrilege had actually been worse than what I was experiencing
with my analyst. I felt that I was being given a chance to redeem
myself, so I was able to feel my desire and consciously hold my position as an equal partner.

During this period, I read Stein's book, *Incest and Human Love*. It resonated in me with a truth that I was not quite ready to face. However, I began to have healing dreams about my father, an alcoholic who had been subjected to incest by his mother. My father had been involved in a series of affairs during my childhood. These affairs were known to myself and my mother. My mother responded with physical and psychic illnesses; I responded as judge, jury, and executioner. The healing dreams that I experienced at this time all expressed that my father was the person to show me the way home. This was difficult for me to accept because my consciousness had always rejected him, though my actions had often been just like his.

During the seventh month of my analysis, my father's wife died of the same type of cancer as had my analyst's wife, which I consider an amazing synchronicity. Watching my analyst's pain created a newly felt compassion in me for what my father must have been feeling. I decided to go home for the funeral. As I discussed the trip with my analyst, I expressed my fear at being with my father for so many days; I was concerned that he would try to upset me as he always had done in the past. Asked how my father had done this, I described my father's overt racism and explained how he would deliberately use racist language to upset me. My analyst responded that my father was "trying to get me hot." As with Stein's book, my consciousness was shaken, but something deeper in me knew this was true.

I returned for the funeral. Things went better than I expected between my father and me. The dreams I had about my father and my experience with my analyst had loosened my attitude, and I felt a new openness to my father.

On my last day, my father offered to visit my mother's grave with me. As we placed flowers on it together, I asked my father to tell me about how he and my mother first met, and what she was like as a teenager. He began with a detailed sexual description of her and how she "got him hot." As he further detailed their sexual escapades, I felt as if he were, however unconsciously, trying to arouse me. I started to feel sick to my stomach. I stopped him, telling him that I felt this was his private life and that I was not interested. However, as I said this, my body's sensations broke into my consciousness. I felt myself starting to lubricate—my body was preparing itself to have sex with my father.

I felt deep humiliation. Yet, I knew that a very deep split was being made conscious. This exchange between my father and myself was a reenactment of the unconscious relationship I had experienced with him during my childhood.

Years earlier, I had become aware of a four-tiered way of relating within myself: erotically, emotionally, intellectually, and spiritually. I related these levels to parts of my body: my erotic level was linked to the lower abdomen; my emotions to the stomach; and my intellect to the head. My spiritual level was felt more as an inner intuitive quality. When I met someone, I would check the feeling of each part to see how I was relating to the other person. Often, one or two areas would resonate. When I met that rare person with whom I felt three levels resonate, I would begin to lose a sense of myself, so strong was the pull to unite.

During my analysis, I began to experience resonance on all four levels for the first time. Because I was able to withstand the desire to merge with and lose myself in the Other, I began to realize that these levels were actual splits within myself. I believe that this splitting occurred very early, as each level developed in me. These splits protected me from being lost in the chaos of my family, but they also prevented me from relating fully to any other human being. Once my incestuous feelings for my father were made conscious, and I was connected with my own feminine healing energy, this four-tiered split united into an open channel that I felt running from my chest area to the chest area of my analyst.

This new resonance satiated the desire for literal merger and created in me a new way of relating that brought my whole being together into my consciousness. Key to this development was our ability to acknowledge and hold the sexual tension between us within a deeply caring environment. The pull for sexual merger was the desire of my unconscious to keep my incestuous feelings unconscious. The erotic transference was the Self's way of creating a possibility for healing. Surrendering to the guidance of the Self created an unfolding series of synchronous dreams and events that led me to a greater wholeness.

The Brother/Sister *Coniunctio*

Once the parental incest split has been healed, the brother/sister *coniunctio* may be approached. An interpsychic healing of the brother/sister split can only occur between equals. Analyst and analysand will know that they are ready to approach this split when each has achieved an awareness of the strengths and weaknesses of the masculine and feminine sides within themselves. This may be experienced as an awareness that each can kill and be killed, devour and be devoured, heal and be healed. A field will be created between, through, and possibly around the couple involved. Intense bodily and psychic feelings will be experienced.[9] The analyst and analysand who are committed to transforming this *prima materia* into the *lapis philosophorum* will not flee from this opportunity. The nymph faces Pan as an equal: unjoined yin and yang with no part of the other yet within.

This is a momentous time. The energies are at critical mass: ecstasy and abyss, creation and destruction, eternity and annihilation.[10] Since the field created between the analytic couple will vary from couple to couple due to the development and uniqueness of each, the specific transforming image or experience will be unique to that couple. However, I would like to offer two images that I have found helpful in holding the tension while awaiting the healing and transformative experience.

The Descent to the Mothers

In Goethe's *Faust*, Faust is instructed by Mephistopheles on the manner in which to call up the spirits of Paris and Helen, who together constitute a symbol of the sacred brother/sister *coniunctio*. Mephistopheles tells Faust that he will travel to the realm of the Mothers:

> I dislike letting out one of the higher secrets. There are goddesses throned in solitude, outside of place, outside of time. It makes me uneasy even to talk about them. They are the Mothers. . . . Goddesses unknown to mortal men, hardly to be named by them.
>
> You'll need to dig deep to reach them. . . . You'll enter the untrodden, the untreadable, the unpermitted, the impermissible. Are you ready? There'll be no bolts. You'll be pushed about from one emptiness to another. Have you any notion what emptiness is? Barrenness? (Edinger 1990)

Mephistopheles then gives Faust a key, a shining, flashing key that grows in his hand. Faust, embracing this phallic symbol, states, "I feel a new access of strength as soon as I grip it firmly. My chest expands. On to the great task."

Mephistopheles then states:

> When you come to a glowing tripod you'll know you're as far down as you can go. By the light it throws you'll see the Mothers. Some sitting, some

standing or walking about. It just depends. Formation, transformation, the eternal mind eternally communing with itself, surrounded by the forms of all creation. They won't see you. They only see ghosts. You'll be in great danger and you'll need a stout heart. Go straight up to the tripod and touch it with your key. That's the way. It'll connect and follow you as your servant. Now you'll calmly ascend. Your good fortune will hoist you. And before they notice, you'll be here with it. And once you have it here you can call up hero and heroine from the shades. You'll be the first to pull it off. It'll be done and you'll have done it. The clouds of incense will turn into gods as part of the magic process and so remain. (Edinger 1990, pp. 54–56)

Faust descends to the realm of the Mothers. He sees the tripod and approaches it with his key. As he gets closer, its power is felt. A vapor rolls in, but Faust presses forth. As he nears the tripod, Paris emerges, a shepherd of uncomparable beauty. Then Helen appears, of whom it is said that "he who beholds her must distracted sigh, he who possessed her won a bliss too high" (Wayne 1969, pp. 86–87). This vision of the *coniunctio* is too much for Faust. He is inflamed with desire. Faust reaches to possess Helen, forgetting his mission; the approach to the Mothers by the phallic symbol was too intoxicating for him. There is an explosion; Faust is rendered unconscious, and the remainder of the play is enacted in the unconscious realm.

The approach to the *coniunctio* is a dangerous one indeed. Tension and emotions run high. Only conscious awareness of the consequences of acting out desire can provide the strength to merely touch the realm of the Mothers. Here again, Phallos must have conscious limits. And the nymph who is in touch with the tripod of the Lilith/Sophia/Aphrodite energies must withhold the destructive, intoxicating vapors and visions if a *coniunctio* is to occur.

The Virgin and the Unicorn

Before reading Rutter's book, I had a dream similar to his encounter with Mia. In my dream, I had awakened feeling as if I had missed an appointment with my analyst. When I arrived, I sat at his feet and placed my head in his lap. He was kissing me and I was loving, but seductive. He stopped me and I returned home, shattered, not knowing who I was.

In my own dream, I experienced the desire to seduce and be seduced, love and be loved, heal and be healed. However, the intrapsychic tension could not be held. Much like the explosion in *Faust*, I felt shattered. No *coniunctio* was achieved.

Shortly thereafter, I came across the alchemical image represented in Jung's *Psychology and Alchemy*, depicting the virgin taming a unicorn (1944, p. 438). In that picture, shown below, a unicorn is being held by a virgin in her lap. Jung described this picture as symbolizing the transformative power of Mercurius. "The virgin represents his passive, feminine aspect, while the unicorn illustrates the wild, rampant, masculine, penetrating force of the *spiritus mercurialis*" (ibid.). This taming of an instinct is shown by a touching, a holding, much like the directions given to Faust by Mephistopheles.

My image and Mia's actions were much like this symbol. Having the ability to hold the tension between the opposites promises a healing and transformative experience.

Virgin taming a unicorn. Thomas Aquinas (pseud.), "De alchimia" (16th cent.) Ms. Voss. Chym. F. 29, f.87r. Reproduced by permission of Leiden, University Library.

Coniunctio

A *coniunctio*[11] may be experienced in a number of ways.[12] The field between the analytic couple may intensify, and an experience similar to psychic orgasm may be felt within the mind, the body, and the soul of each.[13] A healing image may appear within the field, seen as a tantric pair, a radiant light, the couple themselves involved in an embrace, or other images of unity.[14]

The *coniunctio* may also complete itself when the couple is apart. A uniting dream or vision signifying a new masculine/feminine relationship may occur. Often a psychic pregnancy or birth will appear as well.[15]

The *coniunctio* brings with it a new sense of connection to "the Other," the intrapsychic "other," and the other person in the analytic couple. A feeling of resonance is experienced. This occurs because each person becomes aware that the part which each so intensely desired to possess and merge with in the other is also present, and now conscious, within themselves. The open channel that had demanded merger is now felt as an open channel of resonant connection, an experience of grace.[16]

Unfortunately, the *coniunctio* experience is only a beginning. It is a breakthrough. Seeing it otherwise leads only to depression and despair after the experience when life seemingly returns to normal. The *coniunctio* is usually the light at the end of the tunnel, and the experience of it gives hope for a new state of being in this world.

However, much like the baseball player who gets her first hit, there is still much work to do. Old habits die hard. The old conscious matrix, which did not allow the experience of this new conscious "other," must accept this other into the "I" experience. This means reacting in new ways as if this experience of the other is a reality in one's life.[17] Eventually, the experience will become embodied, and a new spontaneity that includes the *coniunctio* awareness will emerge. Experiencing the new contrasexual self, and being this new conscious self, are two different stages.

The embodied *coniunctio* experience creates a new state of being, a new and expanded conscious awareness. It also creates an awareness that consciousness is a finite matrix that fails in light of the infinite.

Opening conscious awareness to the *coniunctio* experience is really opening to creativity and a greater wholeness—a shattering experience to the old consciousness, but the birthing of a new state of being.

Notes

1. Robert M. Stein, M.D., is a practicing Jungian Analyst in Los Angeles. His book, *Incest and Human Love*, and his other scholarly writings have been invaluable to me.

2. Peter Rutter, M.D., is a psychiatrist in private practice in San Francisco. In *Sex in the Forbidden Zone* (1989), he describes sex in the forbidden zone as being "sexual behavior between a man and a woman who have a professional relationship based on trust, specifically when the man is the woman's doctor, psychotherapist, pastor, lawyer, teacher, or workplace mentor" (1989, p. 25).

3. Unfortunately, relationships and marriage often serve the function of avoiding the tension that must be held to make aspects of the contrasexual side conscious and to heal the conscious imbalance of the psyche. The unconscious unwritten contract in many relationships is that the other will hold these aspects of the unconscious contrasexual part that each person needs to consciously develop. Sex and other means of acting out are used as a way of merging with the part that has not been assimilated. Although this may work for a while, the failure of these repetition compulsions to satisfy the intrapsychic imbalance soon creates an emptiness that becomes attributed to the other, rather than to the individual.

4. I recommend Barbara Black Koltuv's *The Book of Lilith* (1986) for a better understanding of this powerful, dark feminine energy within the psyche. The destructive aspects of Pan and the incredible power of Lilith are well known to each other. In this knowing is fear and respect.

5. Sophia, Goddess of Wisdom, knows and respects the penetrating, fertilizing, divine, generative life force of Phallos. For further reading on Sophia, I recommend *Sophia: Goddess of Wisdom* by Caitlin Matthews (1990).

6. Aphrodite, Goddess of Love, is born out of violence and the sea, the ocean within us, the unconscious. Aphrodite, to me, symbolizes the embodiment of love, but a love that has been transformed through suffering and rebirth into compassion.

7. In Woodman's work, the account by Mary entitled "Redeeming Eve's Body" is particularly instructive in the path of experiencing the virgin and the whore split, and uniting them psychically through image and a transforming bodily awareness. Much like the awakening of the kundalini in Eastern awareness, this path provides a cellular transformation and strengthening of the feminine body so that the divine phallos or pneuma may be received. The divine may then be incarnated in matter. This is my understanding of the creation of soul.

8. In retrospect, the warmth surrounding us felt much like the early womblike connection to the mother. When it was abruptly withdrawn, the primal separation experience was relived. My analyst's comment about my seducing him produced in me a deep compassion for his vulnerability, and a humiliation in me for doing something wrong. All of these experiences and emotions seemed to emerge simultaneously.

9. Nathan Schwartz-Salant, in *The Borderline Personality* (1989), gives excellent descriptions of the subtle body-field that can be created. His use of this field is impressive, courageous, and creative. However, it does leave me with a sense of manipulation of the feminine, leading to animus development and *coniunctio* of a sort, but seems lacking in incarnation experience. My feeling is that Schwartz-Salant's inability to surrender to the experience and the ultimate mystery of the sacred *coniunctio* blocks the divine aspect.

10. Much of this is due to an entrenched ego position in a specific gender identification. When we are born, our gender determines many conscious and unconscious reactions to us, which program us with certain beliefs about ourselves and who we are in

reference to our gender. This sets up an unconscious contrasexual self. As differing levels of the brother/sister *coniunctio* are experienced, the conscious self will be experienced as being more androgynous. Aspects of "humanness" will increase as feelings of "otherness" decrease. In addition, more energies and abilities will be accessible to each person.

11. There are many types of *coniunctio* experiences, including the union of opposites that do not involve masculine/feminine energy constellations. Examples of these are the energies manifested as Demeter/Persephone, Apollo/Dionysus, Mercurius/Hermes constellations. These unions involve slightly different issues. I have limited myself in this article to the particular problems evoked in the conjunction of the masculine/feminine constellations.

12. How the *coniunctio* is experienced is also related to the individual's inferior function. Inferior sensates often have intense bodily experiences, where inferior thinking types receive a healing image. The *coniunctio* often comes through the channel least able to defend itself. It then strengthens and develops the inferior function as well, creating a more balanced conscious awareness.

13. Intrapsychic and doubled interpsychic *coniunctio* with a transforming embodiment experience.

14. Intrapsychic and interpsychic *coniunctio*.

15. Intrapsychic *coniunctio*.

16. This channel may be felt in a number of ways, but often it is felt in the body in the area that needs further development. For instance, a chest-to-chest resonance (heart chakra) indicates a breakthrough from the power chakra to the area of compassion. As additional *coniunctio*s are experienced and felt in the body, the individual more deeply feels the area that is blocked and in need of healing. This deep psychic body work is moreover necessary to release damage caused to a child during his or her preverbal development. The resonance releases deep images and feelings that the ego can understand, dialogue with, and assimilate into consciousness.

17. Much needs to be relearned. Memory, before the *coniunctio* experience, did not include this new awareness. Memory largely conditions our reactions to events in our lives. Until memory assimilates the *coniunctio* experience into its repertoire, through practice and discipline, our reactions to events will be the same as they were before the *coniunctio* experience.

References

Bly, R. 1990. *Iron John*. Reading, Mass.: Addison–Wesley Publishing.

Edinger, E. 1990. *Goethe's Faust: Notes for a Jungian Commentary*. Toronto: Inner City Books.

Jung, C. G. 1944. *Psychology and Alchemy. CW*, vol. 12. Princeton, N.J.: Princeton University Press, 1953.

Koltuv, B. 1986. *The Book of Lilith*. York Beach, Maine: Nicholas–Hays.

Matthews, C. 1990. *Sophia: Goddess of Wisdom*. San Francisco: Unwin Hyman.

Rutter, P. 1989. *Sex in the Forbidden Zone: When Men in Power—Therapists, Doctors, Clergy, Teachers, and Others—Betray Women's Trust*. Los Angeles: Jeremy P. Tarcher.

Schwartz–Salant, N. 1989. *The Borderline Personality: Vision and Healing*. Wilmette, Ill.: Chiron Publications.

Stein, R. 1984. *Incest and Human Love: The Betrayal of the Soul in Psychotherapy*. Dallas: Spring Publications.

———. 1991. The fear of the phallos. *Spring* 51:26–32.

Wayne, P. 1969. Trans. Goethe's *Faust* Part Two. Baltimore: Penguin Books.

Woodman, M. 1992. *Leaving My Father's House*. Boston: Shambhala Publications.

Pouring Old Wine into a New Bottle

A Modern Alchemical Interpretation of the Ancient Hermetic Vessel

Steven M. Rosen

Over the past two decades, I have been engaged in phenomenological research that has drawn extensively from topology, an area of modern mathematics dealing with the qualitative properties of surfaces. Specifically, I have examined the characteristics of two paradoxical and highly integrative structures, the Möbius surface and the Klein bottle, and have explored their holistic implications for several fields of scientific and philosophical inquiry (Rosen 1975a, 1975b, 1980, 1987, 1988). In the course of this work, I was more or less vaguely aware of a possible connection with the old hermetic discipline of alchemy but only recently was the relationship brought home to me in a concrete, vivid way.

Steven M. Rosen, Ph.D., is a professor of psychology at the College of Staten Island of the City University of New York. He teaches psychology and philosophy, lectures internationally, and is the author of numerous essays on psychology, philosophy, parapsychology, education, ecology, and theoretical science. He is the author of *Science, Paradox and the Möbius Principle* and a conceptual novel, *The Möbius Seed.*

(Permissions are acknowledged on pp. 140–141.)

In the summer of 1990, I had turned my attention to the quaternity, the question of the fourfold ordering of nature and the psyche, and this led me to C. G. Jung's three volumes on alchemy (Jung 1944, 1955–1956, and *Alchemical Studies, CW,* vol. 13). As my reading of these texts progressed, I was struck by what appeared to be a remarkable correspondence between the paradoxical Klein bottle I had been studying and the enigmatic vessel in which the work of the alchemists purportedly took place.

The present article provides a detailed account of this conjunction. I describe the properties of the hermetic vessel, primarily as brought out by Jung, then turn to the Klein bottle and my "alchemical" interpretation of it. In laying these two structures alongside each other, I believe it becomes clear that their correspondence is more than adventitious, that the coincidence goes beyond a mere superficial resemblance of entities that are essentially different. The paper concludes with a brief postscript on the archetypal significance of pouring "old wine" into a "new bottle."

The Ancient Bottle of Hermetic Tradition

The popular misconception is that alchemy was nothing more than an absurd flirtation with transmuting base metals into gold. Jung's extensive research into the hermetic enterprise did much to dispel this view. His investigations disclosed that the work of alchemy, sustained over many centuries, entailed a serious effort, not merely to transform matter, but the human psyche as well.

Let us begin by taking note of the unique way the alchemist saw the relationship between psyche and matter. In the words of Jung:

> The alchemical *opus* deals in the main not just with chemical experiments as such, but with something resembling psychic processes expressed in pseudochemical language. . . . [I]n alchemy there are two . . . heterogeneous currents flowing side by side, which we simply cannot conceive as being compatible. Alchemy's "tam ethice quam physice" (as much ethical—i.e., psychological—as physical) is impenetrable to our logic. If the alchemist is admittedly using the chemical process only symbolically, then why does he work in a laboratory with crucibles and alembics? And if, as he constantly asserts, he is describing chemical processes, why distort them past recognition with his mythological symbolisms? (Jung 1944, par. 342)

Of course, as Jung well knew, alchemy is "impenetrable to our logic" precisely because our logic separates "hard reality" from that which is "merely symbolic," divides *physis* from *psyche*, object from subject. By contrast, the alchemical object is at the same time subject. Jung took pains to bring this out, speaking of alchemy as both a laboratory procedure and a meditation, referring to alchemical "imagination" as "a hybrid phenomenon . . . half spiritual, half physical" (1944, par. 394). "There was no 'either-or' for that age," says Jung, "but there did exist an intermediate realm between mind and matter. . . . This is the only view that makes sense of alchemical ways of thought, which must otherwise appear nonsensical" (ibid.). In fact, Jung goes so far as to imply that the disciplines of contemporary physics and transpersonal psychology, both of which touch "on an impenetrable darkness," may be reawakening "the intermediate realm of subtle bodies [. . . wherein] the physical and the psychic are once more blended in an indissoluble unity" (ibid.).

Now, the remarkable work of alchemy was to be carried out in a vessel with remarkable properties in its own right. Jung introduced his discussion of the hermetic vessel with these words:

> Although an instrument . . . it is no mere piece of apparatus. For the alchemists the vessel is something truly marvellous: a *vas mirabile*. Maria Prophetissa says that the whole secret lies in knowing about the Hermetic vessel. "Unum est vas" (the vessel is one) is emphasized again and again. It must be completely round . . . (the spherical or circular house of glass). (Jung 1944, par. 338)

Elsewhere Jung speaks of the "house of the sphere" as the "*vas rotundum*, whose roundness represents the cosmos" (1955–1956, par. 373), this "rotundity" being associated with the realization of wholeness; evidently, the "roundness" must be "simple and perfect" (Jung 1944, par. 116). But I suggest that this "perfect roundness" is not fully grasped just by imagining the unbroken surface of a sphere or the circumference of a circle, for, as Jung's studies reveal, the "roundness" of the hermetic vessel is decidedly *paradoxical* in nature.

One indication of this lies in the fact that the vessel was to be *bene clausum*, well closed or "hermetically sealed" (Jung 1944, par. 219). By maintaining the absolute closure of the vessel's surface, the simplicity and perfection of its roundness would be upheld. However, the vessel was also thought of as a sieve (Jung 1944, par. 338), an apparatus with openings in it to allow finer substances to pass through. Apparently, then, the vessel was to be closed and open at the same time!

The way in which this peculiar requirement could be met becomes clearer when a key symbol of the alchemical enterprise is

Figure 1.   The uroboros

taken into account: the *uroboros*, the ancient figure of the serpent
or dragon swallowing its own tail (figure 1). According to Jung,
"Time and again the alchemists reiterate that the *opus* . . . is a sort
of circle like a dragon biting its own tail" (1944, par. 404). Bearing in
mind that the hermetic vessel is not merely a piece of equipment to
be used in the work of alchemy but is identified with that work in a
primary way, we may suppose that the roundness or circularity of
the vessel is itself uroboric in character.[1] So when we see the symbol of the serpent appearing on the vessel (e.g., Jung 1944, par. 404;
Metzner 1971, p. 96; Read 1966, plate 35), we may interpret this to
mean that the vessel's very structure is that of the uroboros. Indeed,
the surface of such a vessel would not merely be closed as is the
surface of a sphere, but open as well. For, while the dragon that has
swallowed itself is contained within its own skin (as it would be in
a closed vessel), at the same time it is ecstatically *un*contained, that
is, beside itself, outside its skin in the open.

Evidence confirming the ecstatic structure of the hermetic vessel is found in its association with the symbol of the pelican. Read illustrates a form of the vessel called the "double pelican" (figure 2a),
which "was mystically connected with the process of conjunction
[the union of opposites]" (1966, p. 149). And Jung, in the course of
describing the Paracelsan version of alchemical transformation as a
retorta distillatio, presents another illustration of an alchemical
container shaped like a pelican. According to Jung, the *retorta distillatio* presumably "meant a distillation that was in some way

Figure 2a.   Double pelican

turned back upon itself. It might have taken place in the vessel called the Pelican [figure 2b] where the distillate runs back into the belly of the retort" (1942, par. 185). Earlier in the same volume, Jung refers to alchemist Gerard Dorn's characterization of the hermetic vessel as the *vas pelicanicum* and further notes:

Figure 2b.   Pelican as vessel and as bird

> The anonymous author of the scholia to the "Tractatus aureus Hermetis" says: "This vessel is the true philosophical Pelican, and there is none other to be sought for in all the world." It is the lapis [the Philosopher's Stone] itself and at the same time contains it; that is to say, the self is its own container. This formulation is borne out by the frequent comparison of the lapis to . . . the dragon which devours itself and gives birth to itself. (Jung 1954, par. 115)

So the curious roundness of the hermetic vessel is embodied both in the uroboros and in the pelican, creatures portrayed as penetrating themselves in such a way that they are inside and outside of themselves at the same time.

In Jung's final major work on alchemy, he develops the theme of the pelican still further:

> In the scholia to the "Tractatus aureus Hermetis" there is a quaternio consisting of *superius/inferius* [upper/lower], *exterius/interius* [outside/inside]. They are united into one thing by means of the circular distillation, named the Pelican. . . . For when she [the pelican] applies her beak to her breast, her whole neck with the beak is bent into the shape of a circle. . . . "Let all be one in one circle or vessel." "For this vessel is the true philosophical Pelican, nor is any other to be sought after in all the world." (Jung 1955–1956, par. 8)

Jung concludes this paragraph by reproducing the diagram of the "circular distillation" that appeared in the original text he has examined (figure 3). He explains that:

> B C D E represent the outside, A is the inside, "as it were the origin and source from which the other letters flow, and likewise the final goal to which they flow back," F G stands for Above and Below. (1955–1956, par. 9)

In Jung's earlier volume, the same illustration appears in a footnote, along with a quotation from the "Tractatus aureus Hermetis" describing the "circular distillation":

> the outside to the inside, the inside to the outside, likewise the lower and the upper; and when they meet together in one circle, you could no longer recognize what was outside or inside, or lower or upper; but all would be one thing in one circle or vessel. For this vessel is the true philosophical Pelican, and there is no other to be sought for in all the world. (1944, par. 167)

For the third time, we encounter Jung's reference to the hermetic vessel as the "true philosophical Pelican," now accompanied by the preceding text which makes it easier to appreciate its self-penetrating, ecstatic character. Referring to the drawing, Jung goes on to comment that the "little circle is the 'inside,' and the circle

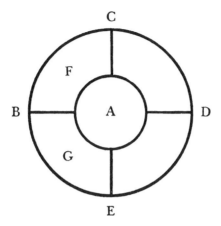

Figure 3.   Circular distillation

divided into four is the 'outside': four rivers flowing in and out of the inner 'ocean'" (1944, par. 167).

In a chapter devoted to examining the many paradoxes of alchemy, Jung offers still another perspective on the vessel. According to Jung, the alchemical paradoxes culminate in the so-called "Enigma of Bologna," which he characterized as "a perfect paradigm of the method of alchemy in general" (1955–1956, par. 88). On an allegedly ancient monument said to have been found near Bologna, there appeared an inscription that concluded with the following passage:

> (This is a tomb that has no body in it.
> This is a body that has no tomb round it.
> But body and tomb are the same.) (Ibid., par. 51)

This seemingly nonsensical text attracted much attention among the alchemists, who meditated upon it and devoted great effort to its interpretation. The mysterious persona for whom the inscription was supposed to have been written was named "Aelia Laelia," and according to alchemist Michael Maier, Aelia herself "is the container, converting into herself the contained; and thus she is a tomb or receptacle that has no body or content in it, as was said of Lot's wife, who was her own tomb without a body, and a body without a tomb" (ibid., par. 64). Jung identifies the enigmatic tomb of Bologna with the hermetic vessel. So we witness again the vessel's ecstatic property: outside ("tomb") and inside ("body") permeate each other as one.

Of particular interest for our purpose is the appearance of the vessel in the material of *glass*. As already noted, it was referred to as the "house of glass," as a "vessel of diaphanous glass" (Jung 1955-1956, par. 261), a "glass vessel that is 'furnished before and behind with eyes' and 'sees the whole universe'" (Jung 1954, par. 114). The symbolic significance of glass is brought out in Jung's association of the hermetic vessel with the Grimms' fairy tale "The Spirit in the Bottle" (Jung 1948, pars. 239-246).

In Jung's view, this story "contains the quintessence and deepest meaning of the Hermetic mystery": a powerful spirit is trapped in the earth beneath an oak tree, enclosed within "a well-sealed glass bottle" (1948, par. 239). Hearing the spirit cry "Let me out!" a passing youth opens the bottle, whereupon the spirit rushes forth, identifies himself as mighty Mercurius, and threatens to strangle his liberator. But the boy tricks the spirit back into the bottle, and the tamed Mercurius then promises that, if freed again, he will serve the boy in a beneficial way.

Jung relates the glass bottle of the Grimms' fairy tale to the hermetic vessel with the following words:

> The bottle is an artificial human product and thus signifies the intellectual purposefulness and artificiality of the [alchemical] procedure, whose obvious aim is to isolate the spirit from the surrounding medium. As the *vas Hermeticum* of alchemy, it was "hermetically" sealed. . . . [I]t had to be made of glass, and had also to be as round as possible, since it was meant to represent the cosmos in which the earth was created. (Jung 1948, par. 245)

In Jung's interpretation, the Mercurial spirit represented to the alchemists the initially unconscious, wildly irrational power of instinct, of embodied nature. In turn, the "bottling up" of Mercurius signified the necessity of gaining intellectual control of nature. But Jung's construal of the problem of freeing Mercurius (1944, pars. 250-251) seems less than complete, and I will venture to carry it further.

The fashioning of the hermetic bottle symbolizes a process of purification which culminates in the *unio mentalis* (see Jung 1955-1956, p. 465), a state of intellectual maturity that is the climax of mental development. This is the challenge symbolically faced by the boy in the Grimms' fairy tale, and the challenge the alchemist faced. Prior to "properly sealing the bottle," Mercurius was always a threat to escape, a regression to the primal past that would overwhelm the alchemist. In the meanwhile, the alchemist had to keep the "spirit" imprisoned as best he could.

Note Jung's observation that "the alchemists rightly regarded 'mental union in the overcoming of the body' as only the first stage of conjunction or individuation. . . . In general, the alchemists strove for a *total* union of opposites" (1955–1956, par. 676). This meant that once mental integration was attained, there would need to be additional "distillations," alchemical processes entailing a reunion of mind with the body, and with the rest of nature. But mental purification had to come first. In this regard, Jung cited alchemist Gerard Dorn: one must "free the mind from the influence of the 'bodily appetites and the heart's affections'. . . . In order to bring about their subsequent reunion, the mind (*mens*) must be separated from the body . . . for only separated things can unite" (1955–1956, par. 671).

As I see it, the secret of fluid passage from the *unio mentalis* to the subsequent stage of reunion with the freed Mercurial body lies in the very structure of the hermetic vessel. What would be discovered up on sealing that bottle in earnest? That it is a *vas pelicanicum*, an *uroboros*. Therefore, at the moment the bottle would be truly sealed, when Mercurius would be closed into it hermetically and no longer able to escape, one would find that the spirit would be outside the bottle as well, now as a beneficial agent of healing, of wholeness. By genuinely completing the vessel, by closing the body within the mind in an "airtight" fashion, the simple containment of body by mind would be overcome and the body set free in union with mind. The body contained within this finished bottle, like the body of Aelia Laelia, would be at once *un*contained ("a body that has no tomb round it").

In sum, the completed hermetic vessel would be a structure that would contain itself, flow through itself, that would be "both content (mother liquid) and container" (Jung 1955–1956, par. 439). The inside and outside of this remarkable bottle would be united paradoxically as a single side.

The Inside-Out Bottle of Modern Topology

As I noted in the introduction, my work with the qualitative mathematics of surfaces long preceded my study of alchemy. The Klein bottle is a curious topological surface named after its discoverer, the German mathematician, Felix Klein. To comprehend this structure, let us first examine its lower-dimensional counterpart, the surface of Möbius. The unique character of the latter is exhibited through the comparison shown in figures 4a and 4b.

A cylindrical ring (figure 4a) is constructed by cutting out a narrow strip of paper and joining the ends. The Möbius surface (figure 4b) is produced simply by giving one end of such a strip a half-twist (through an angle of 180 degrees) before linking it with the other.

The cylindrical ring possesses the conventionally expected property of two-sidedness: at any point along its surface, two distinct sides can be identified. In the Möbius case, it is true that if you

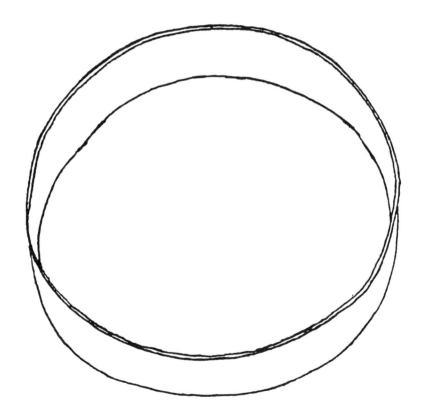

Figure 4a.   Cylindrical ring

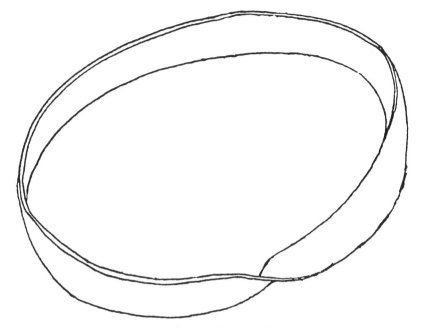

Figure 4b.   Surface of Möbius

place your index finger anywhere on the surface, you will be able to put your thumb on a corresponding point on the opposite side. The Möbius strip does have two sides, like the cylinder. However, this holds true only for the local cross-section of the strip defined by thumb and forefinger. Taking the full length of the strip into account, we discover that points on opposite sides are intimately connected—they can be thought of as twisting or dissolving into each other, as being bound together internally. Accordingly, mathematicians define such pairs of points as *single* points, and the two sides of the Möbius strip as but *one* side. (If the Möbius property of one-sidedness is difficult to imagine in the abstract, it is very easy to demonstrate. For instance, when you draw a continuous line along the whole length of the strip, on returning to your point of departure you will discover that your ink mark has covered both sides of the surface!)

It is important to realize that the surface of Möbius is not one-sided in the homogeneous sense of a single side of the cylindrical ring. It is one-sided in a paradoxical sense, one-sided and also two-sided, for the local distinction between sides is not simply negated with expansion to the Möbius as a whole. When the sides come together, their distinct identities are not merely washed away. The sides of the Möbius remain distinct, yet they also are one and the same.

What is the significance of this topological conjunction of opposite sides? In an earlier work (Rosen 1977), I explored the relationship between Möbius integration and the integration of *psyche* and *physis* (mind and matter, subject and object). Of course, just this marriage of opposites is found in alchemy, in the "hybrid," "half spiritual, half physical" hermetic vessel. However, the true topological counterpart of the hermetic vessel is not the Möbius surface, for the Möbius lacks sufficient dimensionality.

The surface in question is a two-dimensional structure embedded in objective three-dimensional space.[2] What is the dimensionality through which we *observe* this structure? The observing human psyche is not itself extended in three-dimensional space but operates in a fourth, *in*tensive, subjective realm. Therefore, while the Möbius surface indeed may effectively symbolize the *coincidentia oppositorum*, the paradoxical union of object and subject, in itself it is but an object, an entity simply appearing before us in physical space, thus incapable of directly incorporating the inner depths of our psyche. What would be needed to accomplish the latter? Not a two-dimensional body enclosed as mere object in three-dimensional space, but a body of paradox that is itself three-dimensional, one standing open to the fourth dimension.

Enter the Klein bottle. This higher-dimensional counterpart of the Möbius surface does seem to leave the necessary opening for our inwardness. By way of introduction, notice an interesting feature of the Möbius: its asymmetry.

Unlike the cylindrical ring, a Möbius surface has a definite orientation in space; that is, it can be produced either in a left- or right-handed form (depending on the direction in which it is twisted). If both left- and right-oriented Möbius surfaces were constructed and then "glued together," superimposed on one another point for point, the resulting topological structure would be the Klein bottle.

The Klein bottle (figure 5) has the same property of asymmetric one-sidedness as the two-dimensional Möbius, but embodies an added dimension (Rosen 1975a, 1975b, 1980, 1988). Note that we cannot actually produce a proper physical model of the bottle. That

Figure 5.   Klein bottle

is, left- and right-facing Möbius bands cannot be superimposed on each other in three-dimensional space without tearing the surfaces. This inability to objectify the Klein bottle in three-dimensional space derives essentially from the fact that the bottle indeed calls a fourth dimension into play, as we are about to see.

There is a different but mathematically equivalent way to describe the making of a Klein bottle that, for our purposes, will be very instructive. Once again a comparison is called for.

Both rows of figure 6 on the following page depict the progressive closing of a tubular surface that is initially open. In the upper row, the end circles of the tube are joined in the conventional way, brought together through the three-dimensional space outside the body of the tube to produce a doughnut-shaped form technically known as a *torus* (a higher-dimensional analogue of the cylindrical ring). By contrast, the end circles in the lower row are superimposed from *inside* the body of the tube, an operation requiring the tube to pass *through* itself. This results in the formation of the Klein bottle. Indeed, if the structure so produced were cut in half, the halves would be Möbius bands of opposite handedness. But in three-dimensional space, no solid structure can penetrate itself without cutting a hole in its surface, an act that would render the model topologically imperfect. So, from a second standpoint, we see that the construction of a Klein bottle cannot effectively be carried

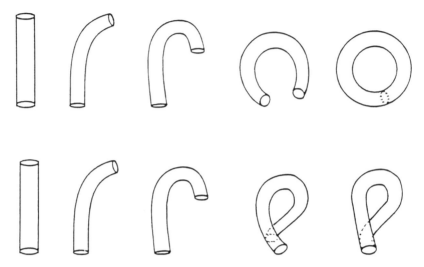

Figure 6.   Construction of torus (upper row) and
Klein bottle (lower row)

out when one is limited to the three dimensions that frame our ordinary experience of external, objective reality.

Now, mathematicians are aware that a form which penetrates
itself in a given number of dimensions can be produced without
cutting a hole if an *added* dimension is available. The point is nicely
illustrated by Rucker (1977). He asks us to imagine a species of "flat-
landers" attempting to assemble a Möbius strip. Rucker shows that,
since the "physical" (i.e., externally experienced) reality of these
creatures is limited to *two* dimensions of space, when they try to
make an actual model of the Möbius, they are forced to cut a hole in
it. Of course, no such problem arises for human beings, who have
full access to three external dimensions. It is the making of the
Klein bottle that is problematic for us, requiring as it would a fourth
dimension. Try as we might, we find no fourth dimension "out
there" in which to execute this operation.

We are now prepared to examine the critical distinction between the standard mathematical interpretation of the Klein bottle
and a modern alchemical one. The crux of the difference lies in the
fact that while conventional mathematics tacitly upholds the split
between *psyche* and *physis*, alchemy aims to overcome it. In the

conventional approach, the concrete subjectivity of the *psyche* is denied and attention limited to the mathematical object. If an object requires three or fewer dimensions for its construction (as in the case of the cylindrical ring, the Möbius surface, and torus), a "real" (i.e., tangibly perceptible) model of it may be fashioned; if the object cannot be assembled in three-dimensional space, objective reality may be extrapolated, extended by an act of abstract imagination in which one or more additional dimensions are summoned. In this view, the "fourth dimension" required to complete the Klein bottle essentially remains an external dimension, albeit an imaginary one, and the Klein bottle is regarded an "imaginary object." Therefore, whether the mathematical object can be concretized or must be approached through abstraction, the conventional mathematician's attention is always directed outward, toward an object; it may take passing note of its own subjective operation, but never will make this its primary focus.

The alchemical approach to the Klein bottle would be decidedly different. Let us look at this difference by placing it in historical perspective.

We know that ancient and medieval alchemy imposed no categorial demarcation of psychological and physical spheres of human experience, but operated in an "intermediary" realm. That "hybrid" mode of apprehension was predominantly pre-rational; that is, it involved a certain absence of discrimination between *psyche* and *physis*, an inability to distinguish the two sharply. It was in this deficient sense that "the physical and the psychic [were . . .] blended in an indissoluble unity" (Jung 1944, par. 394). Just this confusion was reflected in old alchemy's essential difficulty with sealing the "Spirit Mercurius" into the bottle.

Apparently, alchemy itself foresaw what would be needed to address its problem: the perfection of the hermetic vessel in "glass," that is, the further purification of the intellect. How did this *unio mentalis* begin to be brought about? It was effected through the revolution in thinking that occurred with the Renaissance, and the attendant rise of scientific rationalism and modern mathematics. As Berman (1989) recently documented, the first modern scientists were alchemists. Seen from this point of view, the scientific enterprise may be regarded as having originated in the goal of furthering the program of alchemy, not repudiating it. But first things did have to come first. Although *psyche* and *physis* were to be reunited in the end, the process of their hermetic isolation had to be carried forward; for, as alchemist Gerard Dorn said, "only separated things can unite" (Jung 1955-1956, par. 671). Essentially, this meant dividing *psyche* and *physis* in such a way that the old embodied *psyche* that had participated directly in nature (in *physis*) became the coolly objective scientific mind observing nature "out there" as if at a distance, and in the process denying its own primordial origin. Thus, beginning with the Renaissance and for centuries thereafter, individual awareness was directed away from its concrete source, projected outward to an exterior world—a world now witnessed from the detached perspective of the "objective observer."[3] Science devoted itself so single-mindedly to this task of division that it completely lost sight of the unitary aspect of its activity which had been evident at the outset.

But now, in the twentieth century, it appears that the work of science is reaching a point of culmination in which its preoccupation with an objectified *physis* observed from the detached viewpoint of an abstracted *psyche* may be ready to yield, in preparation for the concrete reunion of *physis* and *psyche*. This was Jung's basic reading of contemporary physics.[4] In what specific form appropriate to our modern context will the integration of *psyche* and *physis* become manifested? I suggest it will be expressed as a dimensional integration. That is, *physis*, the dimension associated with extensive, objectified three-dimensional space, will become integrated with a fourth dimension. The latter will not be a dimension that is simply extended before us in the manner of an externalized space, as in the standard mathematical approach. Rather, *physis* will merge with the *in*tensive dimension, that which is folded within us, involving our thoughts, feelings, sensations, and intuitions—the whole of our subjectivity. It will be through this conjunction of outer and inner dimensionality that the new alchemy will consummate the marriage of *physis* and *psyche*.

Again, it is a question of properly fashioning the alchemical vessel. The bottle must be "hermetically" sealed, closed so "tightly" that it is also open; the outer surface of the vessel must be finished in such a way that what lies within it is set free—not merely by being separated from the containing surface but by being integrated with it, thus bringing to fruition the bottle's ecstatically uroboric, inside-out nature ("the outside to the inside, the inside to the outside"; Jung 1944, par. 167). Clearly, the merged "sides" of the completed vessel would not be just the sides of some object appearing out in space, some entity observable to a subject who would remain detached from it. Objectivity and subjectivity themselves would be the "sides" that would permeate each other.

What the modern alchemist can grasp that the ancient alchemist could not is that the merger of objective and subjective sides entails precisely that interpenetration of extensive, external three-dimensionality with our fourth, intensive, interior dimension. Just this *coincidentia oppositorum* is embodied in the one-sided Klein bottle, understood in the light of alchemy. We have seen that the bottle does have an objective side to it, that a palpable model of it can be approximated in three-dimensional space; but we have also realized that it is not simply objectifiable, not an entity like the torus, whose construction in three-dimensional space appears unambiguously completable. That is because the Klein bottle penetrates itself, and, when it is confined to three dimensions, this penetration can only be achieved by cutting it open. Yet, we have also found that the opening which appears in the objective, three-dimensional model of the bottle is filled by introducing a fourth dimension. Interpreting that dimension alchemically, viewing it as the inner dimension of *psyche*, the Klein bottle becomes identified as the present-day counterpart of the hermetic vessel (as even its outward appearance seems to suggest; compare illustrations of the vessel shown in figures 2a and 2b on page 125 with figures 5 and 6 on page 133 and 134). The new incarnation of the bottle, being made of "perfected glass"—constructed in terms of the conceptually mature, highly differentiated idea of mathematical dimensionality—can ecstatically contain the "Mercurial wine" in a way the old bottle could not. When the sides of the Klein bottle fuse, they do so without *con*fusion, without losing their distinctiveness (this was also noted for the sides of the Möbius surface, the bottle's lower-dimensional equivalent). By means of the Klein bottle, outside and inside, *physi*s and *psyche*, are sealed off from one another in such a way that, paradoxically, they totally mesh.

Let me emphasize that the Klein bottle, as hermetic vessel, seals outside and inside from one another *hermetically*; that is, opposing sides are actually differentiated more completely than in conventional structures. The implication here is that the conventional post-Renaissance division of object and subject is by no means a complete division. In viewing an object in the conventional way, we assume that it is complete within itself (a self-standing, simply autonomous entity) by neglecting our own subjective role in the process. In the twentieth century this attitude has come to be called "naive realism." Both in contemporary science (especially theoretical physics) and contemporary philosophy (consider the phenomenology of Husserl, Heidegger, and Merleau-Ponty), recognition has come that the observer and observed are so intimately interconnected that, in effect, they are inseparable. This makes it naive indeed to continue thinking of the observed object as being merely "out there," standing on its own in simple autonomy from the observing subject "in here." By continuing to assume a separation that does not exist and can never be realized, the process of authentic separation is obstructed.

This idea is nicely brought out in Jung's concept of individuation. From the Jungian standpoint, the goal of development is to make the unconscious conscious, to overcome defensive denial and confusion about oneself and gain full-fledged self-knowledge. What the individual is not consciously aware of in himself or herself makes its presence felt *un*consciously, in a deficient, undifferentiated form. Now, the *most basic* impediment to individuation lies in our most basic self-misconception: we mistakenly view ourselves as isolated, simply self-subsistent individuals. For Jung, and indeed for alchemy in general, one completes one's development as a distinct individual only when one recognizes fully the truth of one's intimate entwinement with others, with nature, with the cosmos as a whole. Thus, to be fully individuated means to be fully integrated. Whereas the conventional dualism of post-Renaissance experience achieves neither of these aims, the new alchemy would realize both.

And precisely this thorough differentiation and integration of subject and object is found in the "new alchemical vessel," embodied in the Klein bottle's transpermeation of intensive and extensive dimensions. Without regressively dissolving, each side of the bottle expresses itself *as* the other side and, in so doing, expresses its individuality more truly and fully than in conventional structures such as the torus, which lend themselves to the dualistic "separation" of object and subject that obscures their underlying relatedness. By manifesting the full truth of what they are, the sides of the Klein bottle come into their own, are wholly individuated. Each side is the other side, and each is completely itself, thus completely differentiated from the other side. By virtue of the latter quality, the Klein bottle indeed can be deemed *bene clausum*, "hermetically sealed."

It seems appropriate to end this paper by taking note of the general nature of the work I have done here. It is primarily intellectual work. If the foregoing identification of the old hermetic vessel with the Klein bottle has helped to facilitate an *unio mentalis*, by itself it certainly would not suffice to complete the alchemical *opus*, for, as already intimated, there are deeper orders of the psyche than the intellect, "denser" strata of the subjective dimension that would need to be engaged (viz., feelings, sensations, etc.). In this regard, remember Jung's observation that beyond intellectual development, additional "distillations" are required by alchemy (see p. 129). To quote him further on this:

> The second stage of conjunction, the re-uniting of the *unio mentalis* with the body, is particularly important, as only from here can the complete conjunction be attained. . . . The second stage of conjunction therefore consists in making a reality of [concretely embodying] the man who has acquired some [abstract] knowledge of his paradoxical wholeness. (Jung 1955–1956, par. 679)

What does this mean with respect to the hermetic vessel, the Kleinian medium in which alchemical transformation is to be carried out? I propose it implies that the alchemist must not only *think* the Klein bottle's paradoxical fusion of *physis* and *psyche*, but that this "inside-out" way of thinking must ultimately become a way of *feeling*, *sensing*, and *intuiting*.

So the Klein vessel can be understood as an "object" with an opening perfectly contoured for our subjectivity; a "physical" entity hollowed out to the exact specifications of the psyche. Accordingly, this container properly could be completed, its hole filled, only by going "out" to it through our inner depths, through the hole within ourselves. This is the only way to seal the Klein bottle "hermetically." The very shape and nature of the Klein "object" seems to invite this "subjective" movement, this self-transmutation. Of course, we may decline the invitation, and in that case, the Klein bottle would not have the "extra dimension" it requires to thoroughly express its inside-out character. As a consequence, it would remain but an incomplete model, seen as simply external to us.

Postscript on Archetypes

From the Jungian perspective, we may regard the Klein bottle, *née* hermetic vessel, as rooted in *archetype*. M.-L. von Franz (1975) recounted how, toward the end of his life, Jung saw the need for discovering more universal archetypes, structures he expected would take a mathematical form. Von Franz herself carried this work forward after Jung's death, the research culminating in her book *Number and Time* (1974). Number here is interpreted in a qualitative manner and hypothesized as the primordial organizing principle for the *unus mundus* or "hidden continuum" from which less fundamental archetypes emerge. It is clear from von Franz's subsequent commentary on these efforts that their primary purpose was to promote Jung's ultimate aim of integrating *psyche* and *physis* (1975).

For my part, I would suggest that if archetypes express the underlying unity of *psyche* and *physis*, the most powerful archetype would be one that would go beyond a merely indirect or symbolic expression of this unity to an immediate, fully conscious embodiment of it. A less potent archetype might well symbolically point to said union, but in a manner that implicitly would preserve the division of *psyche* and *physis*, since the split between the archetype as conscious psychic image and the archetype as unconscious, transpsychic ("psychoid") potential would be upheld (the latter being viewed as completely "irrepresentable"; see Jung 1960, par. 840). By contrast, I propose that the Klein bottle, in its four-dimensional realization, would be neither a psychic image nor a material object alone, nor even a linear combination of these, but both *at the same time*—a full-fledged, literal fusion of *psyche* and *physis* giving hermetically differentiated expression to alchemy's "intermediate realm of subtle bodies" (Jung 1944, par. 394).

Notes

1. The literal identification of the alchemical work with the vessel in which it is performed is brought out in a phrase quoted more than once by Jung: "One is the stone, one the medicine, one the vessel, one the method, and one the disposition" (1944, par. 404).

2. For a more technical, detailed treatment of the issue of dimensionality, see Rosen 1988.

3. The interpretation of the Renaissance and its aftermath as a transition from a relatively undifferentiated, concretely participatory mode of consciousness to one that is dualistically detached, accords with a number of writings in cultural philosophy. For examples, see Gebser 1985, Barfield 1988, and Ong 1977.

4. In addition to Jung 1944, par. 394, see Jung 1960, par. 840, and Progoff's discussion of this (1973, chapter 10). See also my own interpretations of Einsteinian relativity and quantum indeterminism, in Rosen 1994.

Permissions

Figure 1 is from C. G. Jung, *Psychology and Alchemy. CW*, vol. 12. Copyright © 1968 by Princeton University Press. Reproduced by permission of Princeton University Press.

Figure 2a is from *Prelude to Chemistry*. Copyright © 1966 by MIT Press. Reproduced by permission of the publisher.

Figure 2b is from C. G. Jung, *Alchemical Studies*. *CW*, vol. 13. Copyright © 1967 by Princeton University Press. Reproduced by permission of Princeton University Press.

Figure 3 is from C. G. Jung, *Mysterium Coniunctionis*. *CW*, vol. 14. Copyright © 1970 by Princeton University Press. Reproduced by permission of Princeton University Press.

Figure 5 is from Martin Gardner, *The Ambidextrous Universe*. Copyright © 1979 by Charles Scribners. Reproduced by permission of the author.

References

Barfield, O. 1988. *Saving of Appearances*. Middletown, Conn.: Wesleyan University Press.

Berman, M. 1989. *Coming to Our Senses*. New York: Simon & Schuster.

Gebser, J. 1985. *The Ever-present Origin*. Athens, Ohio: Ohio University Press.

Jung, C. G. 1942. Paracelsus as a spiritual phenomenon. In *CW* 13: 109–189. Princeton, N.J.: Princeton University Press, 1967.

———. 1944. *Psychology and Alchemy. CW*, vol. 12. Princeton, N.J.: Princeton University Press, 1968.

———. 1948. The spirit Mercurius. In *CW* 13:191–250. Princeton, N.J.: Princeton University Press, 1967.

———. 1954. The visions of Zosimos. In *CW* 13:57–108. Princeton, N.J.: Princeton University Press, 1967.

———. 1955–1956. *Mysterium Coniunctionis. CW*, vol. 14. Princeton, N.J.: Princeton University Press, 1970.

———. 1960. *The Structure and Dynamics of the Psyche. CW*, vol. 8. Princeton, N.J.: Princeton University Press, 1969.

Metzner, R. 1971. *Maps of Consciousness*. New York: Macmillan.

Ong, W. 1977. *Interfaces of the Word*. Ithaca, N.Y.: Cornell University Press.

Progoff, I. 1973. *Jung, Synchronicity, and Human Destiny*. New York: Dell Publishing.

Read, J. 1966. *Prelude to Chemistry*. Cambridge, Mass.: M.I.T. Press.

Rosen, S. M. 1975a. The unity of changelessness and change. *Main Currents in Modern Thought* 31:115–120.

———. 1975b. Synsymmetry. *Scientia* 110:539–549.

———. 1977. Toward a representation of the "irrepresentable." In *Future Science*, J. W. White and S. Krippner, eds. New York: Doubleday/Anchor.

———. 1980. Creative evolution. *Man/Environment Systems* 10:239–250.

———. 1987. Psi and the principle of non-dual duality. In *Parapsychology, Philosophy and Religious Concepts*, B. Shapin, ed. New York: Parapsychology Foundation.

———. 1988. A neo-intuitive proposal for Kaluza-Klein unification. *Foundations of Physics* 18:1093–1139.

———. 1994. *Science, Paradox and the Möbius Principle*. Albany, N.Y.: State University of New York Press.

Rucker, R. 1977. *Geometry, Relativity and the Fourth Dimension*. New York: Dover.

von Franz, M.-L. 1974. *Number and Time*. Evanston, Ill.: Northwestern University Press.

———. 1975. Psyche and matter in alchemy and modern science. *Quadrant* 8:33–49.

VISITING THE MONASTERY—
THEN you must see the horses

Judith Hubback

We saw the Madonna, her bright red dress,
her coal-black face,
> I am black and beautiful;
> my soul is white as snow.
> I am not the scarlet woman.
> > But there is blood on the snow
> > in the steppes of the North
> > and the sand of the South.

and then we saw the silently praying people.
We were all wet from the rain.
It rained and it rained and it rained:
the tears of the world, the whole wide world,
or the tears of God, who knows?

Judith Hubback, M.A., is a training analyst at the Society of Analytical Psychology in London. She is a former psychotherapist for the Student Health Service at University College in London and former editor of the Journal of Analytical Psychology. She is the author of *Wives Who Went to College, Islands and People, People Who Do Things to Each Other,* and numerous other essays and reviews.

Now, quietly, quietly, leave the stress behind,
the cars, the bustle, time and trade,
let us leave all those outside,
though where we live it is dark inside.

Our guide, our monk, arrives:
NOW YOU WILL SEE THE CHOIR,
the paintings of stories we used to know,
and the gilded putti,
the trumpeting angels, miraculous beings,
bodies embodying soulful thoughts,
and so much gilded craft.
                    We're trying to face both soul and body guilt,
                    we gaze, we crane, we hope.

NOW I WILL SHOW YOU THE LIBRARY,
THEN YOU MUST SEE THE HORSES.

Thousands of catalogued books
and the manuscripts of the monks who wrote
with only a single candle:
            Some of the letters are smaller than any I've seen before.
Many of the monks went blind, he tells us,
our guide with the sensitive eyes.

We consider the monks, their amazing devotion
dedication obedience and chill deprivation,
mon pauvre frère, mon riche semblable,
            —but for the grace of God.

GOD IS HERE, our monk is telling us
in his firm and kindly voice,
IN YOU, IN ME, IN NATURE,
GOD IS EVERYWHERE.
        Yes, in the hesitations,
        miscalculations, complications,
        the exaggerations and the painful
        poverty we cannot smell from here,
        also in the generosity, the warm faces,
        the encircling arms—let me hug you,
        you are unhappy.
        Yes, I am unhappy, but it will get better, God is here.

So: NOW YOU MUST SEE THE HORSES
          Why is our monk so keen
          that we should see the horses?

The horses are in the centennial stables,
munching the garnered hay,
breathing well-groomed health.
Their smell is the ancient smell of history.
Then we see the FOALS:
we stand entranced at the beauty of the natural young,
and we try to bring together
our aging bodies and struggling souls,
the past, the present, and the doubtful times to come.
The FOALS will keep the monastery going.

Read in my words what you will,
echoes and fresh ones too,
ma soeur, mon frère, mes semblables.

Now we have seen the mares and the sires,
and we have seen the foals:
also we saw the Black Madonna.
We hope we may find God,
although we have lost the Garden.

Adam and Eve together will go,
tomorrow,
in the morning dew,
to fresh fields and pastures new.

Book Reviews

Analysis Analyzed: When the Map Becomes the Territory
Fred Plaut. London: Routledge, 1993. i–xviii, 1–369. $55.00

Reviewed by Randolph S. Charlton

A new book offers the prospect of a journey into the uncharted territory of another mind. The heft of clean pages, the picture on the dust jacket, the title—all are tantalizing hints at what is to follow. I picked up Fred Plaut's recent book with anticipation. His subtitle, *When the Map Becomes the Territory*, was intriguing. I looked forward to an annotated journey through the vagaries of analytic theory, with time out for visits to the problems of reification and the paradoxical function of analytic maps.

I begin fictional journeys on page one, but when reading analytic theory, before launching myself into a new state of mind, I almost always turn to the back of the book and scan the bibliography for a preview of the territory the author is going to cover. What did I find in Plaut's bookcase? Balint (five references), Bion (seven), Michael Fordham (six), and Melanie Klein (three); psychoanalysts Robert Wallerstein (three) and Donald Winnicott (five); some literary-philosophical figures: Heinrich Böll, Umberto Eco, T. S. Eliot, John Keats, and

Randolph S. Charlton, M.D., is clinical professor of psychiatry at Stanford University Medical School, a Fellow of the American Academy of Psychiatry, and a member of the C. G. Jung Institute of Northern California.

Oscar Wilde; and the author of the Celestial Atlas *Harmonia Macrocosmica* of 1661, A. Cellarius, who was previously unknown to me.

An analyst's professional life proceeds in stages. It begins with the enthusiastic involvement of the trainee, a time during which analytic theories are tried on like so many hats, until one is found that fits and then worn like Holden Caulfield's badge of identity. Then comes a middle period (which for some may never materialize) when the new analyst gets over training and comes to see that the special theory of relativity applies to the psyche as well as the planets. Finally, a well-deserved period of reflection arrives, during which the experienced and now battle-wise analyst reflects on the theory and practice of our impossible profession.

Plaut's book is clearly the product of this last stage of analytic life. The intent of *Analysis Analyzed* is to "clarify what analysis is about." The book is divided into three sections, each offering a view of analysis from a somewhat different perspective.

Part I consists of five chapters that offer cogent insights derived from Plaut's long experience as an analyst. He remarks on the need for an analyst to have faith in faith, and he discusses the limitations inherent in verbal description—especially global-theoretical terms like *the tension of opposites, individuation*, and *transitional object*; the importance of social and cultural context in understanding the products of the unconscious; the mutual nature of the clinical experience; and the difficulty of communicating and evaluating the results of the analytic process. These chapters touch on the experience of consultation with a thoughtful, knowledgeable senior analyst.

Part II, entitled "Learning from Experience," presents an edited and enlarged compilation of Plaut's best previously published papers, most notably "What Do You Actually Do?" and "Object Constancy or Constant Object." The latter offers an excellent and creative summary of early childhood development as well as a Jungian view of how the autonomous psyche can supply a constant object in the absence of object constancy. If you have not read Plaut's thoughts on these issues previously, pick up this book and read them now.

The last chapter in Part II, "The Psychopathology of Individuation," is an interesting springboard to the meaning and use of psychological maps. In an effort to understand the unchanging parts of the personality, Plaut illustrates how psychopathology can be used in the service of individuation. He offers two examples, one biographical and one fictional, to show how two different forms of psychopathology figure significantly in the choice of a constant (idealizable) object. In doing so, he describes a process akin to Kohut's transmuting internalization (p. 184). Unfortunately, the lengthy description of General Charles George Gordon, who sacrificed himself and his men in Khartoum in 1885, and of Celia, a character from T. S. Eliot's seldom-read play *The Cocktail Party,* take the reader on a long and roundabout journey, a journey perhaps worth the time, but one requiring perseverance to understand the form and significance of psychological maps.

Part III, "Analysis Mapped," takes the reader to the heartland of Plaut's cartographic country:

> By making use of an unaccustomed method of graphic representation it is hoped to make recognizable what happens in practice, to make visible the

aims and means of our explorings so that they can become communicable to other interested persons. (p. 270)

The reader is asked to consider whether a pictorial representation of the analytic process can provide information not available in verbal form. The issue centers on the limitation of the way analysts historically communicate. Plaut suggests that verbal description of the clinical situation is inadequate to describe the analytic task; he raises the valid objection that the case illustrations contained in many analytic papers are "all too often designed to support a theory or technique and usually end in a QED." I agree, especially when the conclusion is seen as an incontrovertible truth about human nature. Plaut's conclusion, that case reports are directed prevarications, led him to a search for a more accurate, more telling way of communicating what analysts do and how they think. His knowledge and interest in cartography prompted Plaut to examine the possibility of "mapping" analysis.

"Maps are graphic representations that facilitate a spatial understanding of things, concepts, conditions, processes or events in the human world" (p. 193). Several examples of analytic maps are presented in the book. They are much closer to pictographs or symbolic pictures than the map I use to find my way around San Francisco. Instead of a set of uniform and known signs (roads, geographic representations, shorelines, bridges, and the like), each of Plaut's maps is categorically unique; each uses its own symbols, spatial orientations, and levels of abstraction. Think of a drawing of a dream or a labyrinth or a complex graphical representation of the thoughts of Stephen Dedalus on any particular day in his life.

Plaut does not trust words much. He states, "We have seen that it is next to impossible to describe the fleeting experiential moment of analysis" (p. 194), and he doubts the usefulness of written presentations of clinical material, for such "descriptions are inevitably fused with the point of view of the author."

This last is most certainly true, especially when theoretical jargon is reified and presented as ultimate truth. Yet, *The Sun Also Rises* is fused with Hemingway's point of view, as *Pride and Prejudice* and *Anna Karenina* are fused with the point of view of their authors. Of course, these are works of "fiction," yet it is possible that the language of inventive narration closely approximates the language of the human soul. We have need of an objective geography of the human heart, but perhaps that too is but another fiction.

Naive about the science and art of mapmaking, I find the book's examples of "thematic" and "interactional" maps to be idiosyncratic and almost incomprehensible without the lengthy verbal "key" Plaut thankfully provides. One picture may be worth a thousand words, but though I am an experienced analyst, I could not understand these maps without Plaut's thousands of (very useful) words of explanation. But, please, don't take my word for this; there is food for thought here. The interested reader should look firsthand at these maps to decide on their usefulness for himself or herself.

Donald Spence has suggested that narrative truth and historical truth are not contiguous; Roy Schafer has written about the importance of renarrating an analysand's life; I am sure that Spence, Schafer, Plaut, and I would all agree that a seamless case report bears as much resemblance to reality as a comic book does to an actual life, but Plaut carries a great deal further his objection to the use of verbal communication and clinical narratives. He writes, "an analyst's working method or technique is of no interest to others unless it is meant to advance or bear out a point of theory."

Here I disagree with Plaut. I find that narrative truth has inherent value beyond its historical, theoretical potential. An important aspect of successful analysis is the joint re-creation of a narrative identity for the analysand, an identity best evaluated in terms of internal consistency, external fit, personal meaning, and value. The difficulty in finding the words to say what happens at the quintessential moment of analysis is not reason enough to discard or *overly* distrust narrative case presentations. There is innate value in narrative truth, which can both overlap objective theoretical truth and simultaneously carry its own meaning.

Plaut suggests that graphic representations could allow for a more objective, better differentiated view of analysis. However, would we not still be confronted with the bias of the mapmaker? Can the geography of the human mind be rendered as objectifiable as the Costa del Sol? Even there, the mathematics of fractals suggest that all coastlines are never-ending for there is always another level, always more to see and know—it all depends upon the magnification of the observer's lens.

Essayist W. H. Gass wrote these most memorable words:

> There have been thousands of different drawings of the world, many maps made of reality. Each puts the gods, the good, the false and the true in a different place. They cannot each be correct—there are too many contrary claims—yet society after society has sailed to greatness (not simply the doom they also doomed themselves to) following these false charts, these fictions that have been projected on the planet. (1987)

Perhaps it is my "romantic" nature, perhaps my psychological type, but I don't read Tolstoy, Sherwood Anderson, or Stephen King to advance or bear out my own theories of human nature. Not do I read Jung, Freud, or Winnicott primarily for this reason, though sometimes a particular theory strikes a chord of validity for a given personal or clinical experience.

Case descriptions remain evocative and useful to formulate and communicate my experience and understanding of the process of analysis; and, while I find Plaut's use of graphical images interesting and obviously of great value to him in working out new ideas and relationships between apparently dissimilar situations, I do not understand how such maps would be more objective or informative than verbal descriptions. For me, narrative description and honestly portrayed case material, including unexpurgated, verbatim transcripts, remain the most telling way to communicate what analysis is all about.

Analysis Analyzed is an interesting and thought-provoking book. Plaut's ideas about maps offer us a potentially new way to view and communicate analytic theory, but I am not sure we need a new way. If we do, I'm not sure this is it.

Reference

Gass, W. H. 1987. Review of *The Counterlife*, by Philip Roth. *New York Times Book Review*. 4 Jan., p. 1.

**Imagination as Space of Freedom: Dialogue Between the
Ego and the Unconscious**
Verena Kast. New York: Fromm International Publishing Corporation, 1993.
201 pages. $19.95

Reviewed by August J. Cwik

Jung's work reintroduces the importance of the imagination into modern depth psychology. The "talking cure," with its emphasis on logical, left-brain analysis and interpretation tends to undervalue the imaginal level. Through direct contact with images, Jung's technique of active imagination sought to help the individual to develop a working relationship of the conscious mind to the unconscious mind. Yet, given the absence of a single paper on active imagination at the recent international congress focusing on the transcendent function, one might assume that the field has once again eluded the importance of the imaginal. Verena Kast's book corrects this lopsided situation by reinstating the importance of imaginal work, in the therapeutic situation and in the health of the individual.

Kast's book, written in nontechnical jargon similar to Johnson's chapter on active imagination in *Innerwork*, is as much a cookbook as a Jungian is ever likely to write. Speaking of self-images, she clearly states her basic assumption as "our images always say something about ourselves, they always refer to ourselves, but they may also add to the image by including factors of which we are not yet conscious, and thereby bring about a change in our moods and energy levels" (p.31). Kast nicely demonstrates her working style and interactions with clients through numerous examples. Through guided imaginings, such as the house and tree motif, she shows how to teach people "who do not use their imaginations spontaneously." As she says, "My pointers for the training of imaginative faculties are, of course, addressed to people who are not spontaneous imaginers yet have the wish to establish closer contact with interior images and the transformation processes connected with them" (p. 32). As simple as it sounds, this is exactly the perspective that has been sorely missing in literature on active imagination. Jung emphasized the extreme importance of active imagination because it "gives the patient the inestimable advantage of assisting the analyst on his own resources, and of breaking a dependence which is often felt as humiliating. It is a way of attaining liberation by one's own efforts and of finding the courage to be oneself." Yet the expectation is that the technique be performed alone, as if the patient is supposed to absorb this complicated method by some kind of psychic osmosis. Kast's methodology provides no less than a developmental approach to gaining access to the imaginal activities of the mind.

August J. Cwik, Psy. D., is a clinical psychologist, hypnotherapist, and Jungian analyst in private practice in Chicago. He is a member of the Senior Adjunct Faculty at the Illinois School of Professional Psychology.

Kast's most detailed chapter enumerates a plethora of intervention strategies to assist either the individual's ego or the therapist to engage conflictual
inner images. She gives examples on facing terrifying images, finding helpful
companions, recognizing patterns of relationship or recognizing the wise old
man and woman, and dealing with animals and obstacles. Specifically, she suggests a number of possibilities in dealing with threatening images: attempt to
recognize just exactly what quality is so threatening, address the aspect of the
image that possibly inspires confidence, resolve the conflict by direct confrontation or cunning, take flight when appropriate, use magical means or objects, and begin to open the circle of fear by various interventions. These tac-
tics are informed by and gleaned from an understanding of fairy tales. What
Kast purports to present here is a kind of *logic of the imaginal* based on archetypal understandings. At her best in this type of amplification of imaginal
patterns, Kast argues for their importance in the therapeutic encounter by
stating:

> I have tried to demonstrate how, in the therapeutic process, the therapist
> may assume the ego function of the analysand. A learning process then en-
> ables the analysand to deal with these interior figures, and the ego's ability
> to control is strengthened. This, in turn, makes it possible to detach the
> ego complex from the parental complexes, to distinguish between I and
> not I, to facilitate an examination of these aspects. As paradoxical as it may
> seem, it is precisely by means of this examination, made possible when the
> analyst puts his or her ego functions at the analysand's disposal, that the
> analysand's ego structure can be improved and strengthened; this results
> from its experiencing the ego complex, detached from the parental com-
> plexes as befits the person's age, as increasingly more coherent. A good
> sense of identity arises out of this: the ego is no longer restricted in its
> functions, and defense mechanisms can be employed in a modulated fash-
> ion appropriate to the situation. (p. 173)

Kast naturally assumes that the analyst's suggestions arise from the therapeutic field, in what she calls an "archetypal countertransference [in which] the
analyst, reminded of symbolic material related to the analysand's situation,
places that situation in a larger context" (p. 45). When things proceed well, this
certainly must be the situation: a well-timed imaginal intervention helps the patient to move and grow as described above by Kast. Yet, I have found that the
most common mistake in joint imaginal activity is the tendency too quickly to
come to the aid of the patient and give a suggestion to resolve a conflict. The
individual never gets to bear the anxiety of the conflict and perhaps find his or
her own creativity, Self, in a transcendent resolution. In describing the ethical
confrontation of the ego with an inner figure Jung once said, "Since the way to
agreement seldom stands open, in most cases a *long conflict will have to be
borne*, demanding sacrifices from both sides." This long conflict which must be
borne is at the heart and art of imaginal work: Can these strategies be taught or
must they be discovered anew by each and every imaginer? Sometimes the
best we may be able to do for a patient is to provide the space and support
necessary to help bear the burden. Following a comment made by Winnicott
regarding the interpretive skills of the analyst, perhaps it is not so important

that the analyst be bright and knowledgeable about archetypal understandings, but that he or she can keep it a secret from the analysand.

On the whole, *Imagination as Space of Freedom* is an easily read, enjoyable venture into working with imaginal material in a dyad. All too rarely do we ever get a very real sense of what an analyst says and does in a therapeutic encounter, so it is a pleasure to hear such detailed accounts. Kast's tackling of positive and relaxing fantasy, as being nothing but wishfulness, verges on the poetic. She prefers to call these fantasies images of "longing" and strongly argues for the need for hope in psychic awareness:

> To hope is not simply to build castles in the air: it is, finally, a confidence in life's ability to support us, confidence that all of life and one's intentions can be brought into shared context, even in the future. (p. 17)

She states that such thinking is not necessarily grandiose and that "the imagination always contains unredeemed future—a future that can be redeemed" (p. 54). Kast also has an interesting chapter on dealing with body symptoms and using imaginal techniques to dialogue with the body. The body is all too often left out of the therapeutic encounter, and Kast presents a very real way of getting it back into analysis. She should also be complimented on her integration of behavioral techniques—specifically, relaxation and thought stopping—into imaginal work. She emphasizes that relaxation training can be helpful in itself, but also can be used to deepen access to the emotional life. The attempt to stop negative thoughts and fantasies when they threaten to overwhelm the ego is also an important concept and strategy in analysis. These are the thoughts that lead to nowhere, passive fantasies that only result in persecution and depression. Perhaps conceptualizing imaginal work and active imagination in general as either trance or as an altered state of consciousness might further deepen our understanding of the dynamics of these processes.

If the ability to perform active imagination is as important a goal for the termination of analysis as Jung has suggested, then we need to be more conscious of the use of imaginal activities in our therapeutic work. Kast provides an excellent framework for providing a pathway from joint imaginal work to active imagination proper. This approach has been sadly lacking in the literature. In the future we might need to look more closely at the impact of imaginal activity in therapy on the transference/countertransference situation, and how imaginal work might promote ego-strengthening and detachment in a structural sense while providing groundwork for the formation of the transcendent function.

The Two Million-Year-Old Self
Anthony Stevens. College Station: Texas A & M University Press, 1993. 140 pages. $24.50

Reviewed by James Wyly

In his new work, *The Two Million-Year-Old Self,* Anthony Stevens elaborates a figure of speech coined by Jung to produce a short but far-flung exploration of some implications of the Jungian idea of archetypes for the treatment of psychopathology. Stevens has already written at least as clearly and persuasively as anyone about the logical impossibility of discussing the psyche without assumptions (explicit or otherwise) that parallel Jung's theory of biologically determined archetypes. His *Archetypes: A Natural History of the Self* (1982) remains, in my view, the essential work on the subject after Jung's own. *The Two Million-Year-Old Self* is an application of the ideas of the earlier work to a rather facile remark of Jung's:

> Together the patient and I address ourselves to the two million-year-old man that is in all of us. In the last analysis, most of our difficulties come from losing contact with our instincts, with the age-old unforgotten wisdom stored up in us. And where do we make contact with this old man in us? In our dreams. (Jung 1971)

This "two million-year-old man," Stevens tells us, is a personification of an archetypal unit of the psyche, as are the anima, the shadow, and the wise old man and woman:

> The two million-year-old was another such personification: this archaic presence does not have a physical existence inside our heads, any more than the "soul" or the "unconscious," but as the phenomenological embodiment of our evolutionary inheritance, it can be understood as playing an indispensable role in the drama of our personal lives, "personating" as a companion whom it is possible, as I have learned, to recognize, cherish, and befriend. (p. 4)

Stevens elaborates the concept as one that takes us beyond recorded history,

> back to the hunter-gatherer existence for which our psyches were formed, back to the archetypal foundations of all human experience, back to the hominid, mammalian, and reptilian ancestors who live on in the structures of our minds and brains. To do this is to discover, within Jung's two mil-

---

James Wyly, Psy.D. is a clinical psychologist and Jungian analyst in private practice in Chicago. He is the author of *The Phallic Quest: Priapus and Masculine Inflation.* He holds advanced degrees in both psychology and music and frequently writes and lectures on the relationship between psychology and the arts.

lion-year-old person, a 140 million-year-old vertebrate, which supports our finite existence and animates our dreams. (p. 5)

This is an appealing image upon which to base psychological speculations. Stevens proceeds to do so by grounding his argument in the archetypes as "the basic concept of Jungian psychology." He then demonstrates that, in spite of claims to the contrary, some kind of assumption of archetypes underlies much of the anthropological, psychological, psychiatric, and linguistic thought of our time. He makes a strong and clear case, which leads to the following statement of the question the book addresses:

Nature speaks to us directly in dreams and myths. In our dreams we enter the natural work of our kind: it is the archetypal world, and the archetypal world is the natural world of the dreamer. In dreams we enter the paleolithic caves of our ancestors, and, God help them, bring them up-to-date.

What do our ancestors make of the contemporary world? Much of it, I suspect, they rather like—the ready availability of food, drink, comfort, entertainment, and sexual gratification. But they miss the close ties of kinship, the intimacy of small-community life, the shared responsibilities of hunting, gathering, and defense, the working interaction with nature, the rites and rituals, the myths and legends of heroes, gods, and goddesses, and the magical sense of living in an animated world. Sometimes the disparity between their world and ours is more than they can bear, and they break down and become ill. (pp. 30–31)

The bulk of the book is an expansion of these sentences. Stevens finds "phylogenetically ancient structures" playing important roles in contemporary dreams (p. 37) and argues that dreams "relate the individual to the life cycle of the species" (p. 42). He cites two cases in some detail that lead him to state "a basic principle of psychopathology: Psychopathology results when the environment fails, either partially or totally, to meet one (or more) basic archetypal need(s) in the developing individual" (p. 68). These basic archetypal needs turn out to be the (hypothetical) needs of the two million-year-old person, which Stevens enumerates (pp. 66–67), and which reflect the circumstances in which he supposes late Paleolithic hunter-gatherer communities lived. In other words, the book's point is that psychopathology is the inevitable result of our not living substantially as we believe our ancestors to have lived ten thousand and more years ago.

By attending to the paleolithic inner world, we can not only further our personal individuation but make our own contribution to redressing the gross imbalances of our culture. . . . If many of our psychic ills are due to the frustration of archetypal intentions by the circumstances in which we now live, what may we do about making the two million-year-old man or woman within us feel more at home in the contemporary world?

We can drastically reduce the world's population over the course of the next two centuries; reverse the rabid destruction of natural habitats and the ecosystem; reestablish the centers of human life in small, mutually supportive communities; promote a reverential attitude to all creation; allow a new mythic or religious orientation to emerge, enabling us to see ourselves as the servants of nature rather than the masters. The list is end-less. (p. 119)

There is some appeal in this; but one cannot avoid noticing that what began as an exposition of an archetypal pattern has become essentially an argument for abandoning a hefty portion of our psychological evolution and the cultural heritage we have accumulated since the end of the last ice age. This happens because there is an unspoken and not altogether defensible assumption behind Stevens's conception of the two million-year-old person. His fantasy of the needs of the two million-year-old presupposes an archetypal personality of a staggeringly conservative nature and an overwhelming amount of intrapsychic influence. From Jung's personification of the archetypal substrata of the psyche, Stevens has extrapolated the idea that its essential core is rigidly fixed in the Paleolithic age. Psyche would appear to want nothing beyond the physical and psychological environments of those times; indeed, it would appear unable to assimilate anything else. The archetypes' incapacity for evolution or change seems reminiscent of Kronos at the height of his power. I am inclined to doubt that Jung's fantasy two million-year-old was based on any such assumptions, and even if he had been talking about a Kronos-like figure, his discussion would have had to include the emergence of Kronos's children and the mythological evolution that their appearance implies.

Stevens's argument has probably been unduly colored by the one-sidedness of our time. As he points out, we are overidentified with the heroic, what Stevens calls the "agonic" mode, which has led us to trivialize disastrously the nature we have inherited from our remote ancestors. But this does not mean that a viable solution is to be found in enantiodromia, a reversion to Stevens's "hedonic" hunter-gatherer cultural esthetic. Yet, this is essentially where Stevens leaves us.

Stevens thus ends by articulating a pair of archetypally based opposites one of which he clearly regards as more desirable than the other. This is probably an inevitable stage in dealing with opposites, but a more developed Jungian position would be to avoid value judgments and sustain the oppositional tension, until there emerges a third point of view transcendent to it. I suspect that in our present civilization we can find the seeds of this transcendent place if only we look for them, and that it is in this kind of development, rather than in an attempted return to a fantasized ideal of a distant past, that the further individuation of our culture is to be found. Stevens makes a contribution toward this goal inasmuch as he has articulated the irreconcilable opposition that the widespread psychopathology of our time demands that we transcend.

References

Jung, C. G. 1971. *Psychological Reflections: A New Anthology of His Writings, 1905-1961.* J. Jacobi, ed. London: Routledge & Kegan Paul.

Stevens, Anthony. 1982. *Archetypes: A Natural History of the Self.* London: Routledge & Kegan Paul.

The Political Psyche
Andrew Samuels. London and New York: Routledge, 1993. 380 pages.
Hardcover, $50.00; paper, $16.95

Reviewed by Soren R. Ekstrom

It may seen odd for a well-established analyst to delve into the ephemeral world of politics and our attitudes toward it. However, accompanied by Andrew Samuels, a Jungian analyst in London, the step seems quite logical. The author of the first substantial attempt to describe the development of different schools within the Jungian community after Jung, he has an eye for contemporary social reality. Conversant with how ideas move to form consensus or conflict, Samuels is a sharp observer of what for many of us may seem absolutely irrational and haphazard.

Some of the material in his new book, *The Political Psyche*, is already familiar to readers of the *Journal of Analytical Psychology* (1992: 1,2) and to those who participated in the New York conference on anti-Semitism organized by the C. G. Jung Foundation in 1989. The various papers delivered at this conference, including Samuels's contribution in a shorter version, were published under the title *Lingering Shadows: Jungians, Freudians and Anti-Semitism* (Boston and London: Shambhala, 1991).

The scope of Samuels's investigation of politics has now been expanded by lengthy discussions of prevailing attitudes in several areas, from the men's movement and sexual politics to biases in object relations thinking and the misunderstood role of the father in a child's development. He has also included the results of a questionnaire that he sent to over two thousand analysts and therapists worldwide—Jungian as well as non-Jungian—concerning attitudes toward political material presented in the analytic setting.

His new book consists of three parts. The first, called "the political psyche," discusses the common disgust with politics and attempts to resacralize culture. The second deals with what Samuels calls "the political person," the role of fathers and paternal consciousness in contemporary life. The third part specifically covers the attitudes of analysts and therapists to politics, and is called "the political therapist."

To a Jungian reader, the basic thesis of the book is simple: politics is a transpersonal, thus archetypal, activity; as such, it puts us in contact with a larger social perspective and ought to be seen as an important aspect of who we are. But in psychotherapy a taboo has developed which instructed both therapist and patient that politics do not belong. Is this justified, and how much is it a conscious bias of analysts and therapists?

Samuels's own attitude is presented in the earlier part of his book, and conforms to a general trend among analysts and therapists to view the context

---

Soren R. Ekstrom, Ph.D., is a clinical psychologist and Jungian analyst practicing in Cambridge, Massachusetts.

of a person's life to be as important as the private domain of one's inner life. He writes:

> Political involvement can certainly be a means of avoiding personal con-
> flicts or acting out such conflicts, leaving others to do the changing. But
> political involvement can surely also be a means of expressing what is best
> in humans, acknowledging the fact of our social being, that we are not the
> isolated, solipsistic monads that some psychological theories might lead us
> to believe we are. (p. 14)

Presenting his own attitude is not Samuels's sole ambition, however. He wishes, without a great deal of apology, to continue Freud's search to under-stand "the riddle of the world" and the questions and possible answers, which he arrives at in the beginning of the book, are echoed in his extensive question-naire. Should thoughts and feelings about politics be regarded as mere projec-tions of feelings about self, when they are discussed in the analytic setting? Is it not a shortcoming of therapy or analysis not to permit political issues to have their own validity, without reductive interpretations? How much value does a typical analyst today place on political issues, and how does such an analyst view these issues as they arise during sessions?

For this reader the answers to Samuels's questionnaire, and the discussion of them, are the book's main strength, and there are real surprises in what the questionnaire produced. Of the two thousand people questioned, more than six hundred replied, and their answers were often detailed and highly informa-tive. If we had expected to see old and stereotypical attitudes restated, the sur-prise is even greater. Although a majority of respondents were forty-five years old, they seem to confirm an increased willingness to discuss political issues with their patients. Sixty-seven percent of the respondents had been politically active themselves, and nearly a third said they were politically active at present.

The other parts of *The Political Psyche* are far less exciting. Covering a range of typical attitudes toward politics, the discussion never penetrates be-neath the surface. We miss the deeper redemptive or tragic dimensions in these contemporary preoccupations. Instead, the first parts read more like a commentary for bright and like-minded people, a lament, perhaps, for how lit-tle outlet political idealism seems to have today.

The political dimension of the psyche must be understood to include all the ways we contribute, passively and actively, directly or indirectly, to deci-sions that affect others and ourselves—be they short or long term, global or local, within families, professions, or regular civic life. So wide is the area, and so far-reaching the implications, that it is impossible to cover it all in one book and a few formulations. Samuels's answer to this dilemma is to paint in broad strokes. By entering the ongoing debate on issues discussed in more in-tellectually inclined circles, he may have hoped to demonstrate his thesis more clearly. The problem, unfortunately, is that depth and specificity have had to be sacrificed.

On his home turf of Jungian analysis, psychotherapy, and the history of psychoanalysis, Samuels's arguments are far more convincing, and his dry and somewhat pedantic style detracts less. The result of his questionnaire on poli-tics and psychotherapy is a must for those in the profession. Equally imperative is a review of his discussion of Jung's relationship to Nazi Germany, especially for those who wish to deny the opportunistic ambitions behind Jung's pro-Aryan and anti-Semitic statements. Samuels has unmistakable intellectual honesty, which makes his book important reading.

Integrity in Depth
John Beebe, Foreword by David H. Rosen. Carolyn and Ernest Fay Series in Analytical Psychology. Number 2. College Station: Texas A & M University Press, 1992. Pages i–xxi, 1–165. $19.95

Reviewed by Henry Abramovitch

Analytical psychologists often speak of integration, but perhaps do not consider frequently enough its cognate: integrity. John Beebe's exciting and pioneering work calls upon us to do just that, namely, to consider the depth psychology of how to take responsibility. Jung and his early exponents explored the archetypal dimensions of human experience primarily in two realms: in the Family, with the archetypes of the Great Mother, the Divine Child, the Son-Lover, the Puer Aeternis, and others; and in archetypes of the Self such as the Shadow, the Animus/Anima, and the numinous "coming together of the opposites." Recently, certain authors have drawn attention to other archetypal constellations, for example, Theodore Abt's exploration of the archetype of Home in *Progress Without Loss of Soul*.

Likewise, *Integrity in Depth* breaks new archetypal ground. Beebe makes a convincing case that one's sense of integrity is based on an archetypal experience. He does so by linking the sense of moral wholeness with the bodily sensation of being "upright"—the inner sense of "standing tall" that the upright body-image conveys. The book derives the term for "integrity" from Sanskrit and Latin, but biblical Hebrew may be used just as well to show how physical posture and moral position are fused: the Hebrew word *yashar* means, both literally and symbolically, "straight" and "upright." The Latin root, *integ*, means "not touched," and indeed Beebe argues that "until it is in danger of being compromised, we hardly recognize integrity as a fact of our nature"—that something which should remain inviolable has been touched and violated. Here, Beebe is not speaking of "a fantasy of violation fertile for exploration," one that is "best handled by a metapsychology like Freud's or an archetypal psychology like Hillman's" (p. 19); instead, Beebe speaks of what "the earlier Freud recognized and then abandoned, a literal violation that demands concrete response" (ibid.). Indeed, Beebe suggests a new paradigm for psychotherapy that consolidates the

---

Henry Abramovitch is a Jungian analyst practicing in Jerusalem. He teaches at the Tel Aviv Medical School, is chairman of the Israeli Anthropological Association, and has advanced degrees from Yale University. He is the author of numerous articles and a book, *The First Father.*

work of Kohut, Langs, and even Masson, not as pleasure and displeasure, or ego-Self, but rather as integrity and violation.

In the very first page of his work, while in search of "A Psychological Definition of Integrity," Beebe sets the ethical-literary tone:

> Of the qualities we seek in ourselves and in each other, surely integrity is among the most important. One measure of our need for it may be that we rarely allow ourselves an examination of the concept itself. To do so would be to betray an unspoken philosophic, poetic, and psychological rule of our culture: not to disturb the mystery of what we desire most. Clarification would threaten integrity, a word used like a magic spell to protect what is purest in us from danger. (p. 5)

In seeking to clarify that "state of grace" known as integrity, Beebe gives us a comprehensive look at the heroes of and spokespersons for integrity: Cicero, who may have coined the term; the "Te" component of the Tao Te Ching; the positive pole of Milton's puritanism; and Jane Austen's "quintessential expression of a feminine view of integrity" as constancy (p. 75).

The book discusses "The Shadow and Integrity," "Integrity and Gender," and, finally, "Working with Integrity." There are discussions of how rage, inferiority, and the dream may act as guardians of our integrity; or, how the first step in working with integrity is to "work through our ambivalence about being advised to do so." There are a few poignant clinical vignettes and a delightful retelling and analysis of the story "The Three Army Surgeons," by the Brothers Grimm, which is used as a parable for the centrality of clinical containment for the achievement of integrity. For the most part, though, Beebe explicitly lets the reader do the work of supplying a situation that "allows you to wonder whether you have acted with integrity" (p. 34). The reason this approach works is that throughout this beautiful book, one gets a clear sense of Beebe's own relentless self-inquiry, the bedrock of his own integrity. This discussion of the dynamics of responsibility is welcome, since analysts carry cultural projections as guardians of personal integrity, while, at the same time, leading figures in psychoanalysis, including Jung himself, have been accused rightly or wrongly of violating its sanctity.

This volume is the second in an exciting new series, the Carolyn and Ernest Fay Series in Analytical Psychology, which is produced at Texas A & M University Press. The first was Verena Kast's *Joy, Inspiration, and Hope.* These volumes are superbly produced, and combine scholarly devotion—Beebe's book has more than two hundred fascinating footnotes—with the clarity and originality of a moral virtuoso. John Beebe has constructed for his reader a pathway into the paradox, the mystery, the anxiety of integrity; the question remains whether that reader is man or woman enough to follow.

Q U A D R A N T

"Quadrant is the most important and successful attempt yet to establish links between Jungians and the wider community.... As the crucial contribution of analytical psychology and Jungian thought comes gradually to be recognized, the need for such a journal has become urgent. If Quadrant did not exist, it would have to be created."

—Andrew Samuels, author and internationally known Jungian analyst

"Quadrant emphasizes, in a most creative way, the cultural foundations of Jung's psychology. Its content and format make for exciting reading."

—Thomas Kirsch, president, International Association for Analytical Psychology

The Journal of Contemporary Jungian Thought

Quadrant, the semiannual journal of the C.G. Jung Foundation for Analytical Psychology of New York, presents leading writers and thinkers who offer provocative views of a world poised between inner experience and outer reality.

Quadrant invites you to join in exploring the growth of Jungian thought and its relation to the psychological realities of individuals and society today. Subscribe to Quadrant!

. . . .

To subscribe to Quadrant, detach this form and send it with your payment to:

Ablex Publishing Corporation
355 Chestnut Street
Norwood, NJ 07648

Add $7.50 per year on subscriptions mailed to Canada and overseas.

☐ New
☐ Renewal
☐ Gift

☐ One year ($25)
☐ Two years ($48)
☐ Three years ($69)

Please enclose your check or money order.

Name _____

Address _____

_____

City/State/Zip

Message for gift subscription card:

_____

_____

Harvest
Journal for Jungian Studies
1994, volume 40.
Editor: Renos Papadopoulos

Correspondence for the Editor:
20 Woodriffe Road,
London E11 1AH